ALSO BY DIANA ATHILL

Fiction

An Unavoidable Delay
Don't Look at Me Like That

Memoirs

Stet
Instead of a Letter
After a Funeral
Yesterday Morning
Somewhere Towards the End
Life Class (omnibus)

Letters

Instead of a Book

Make Believe

Diana Athill

GRANTA

Granta Publications, 12 Addison Avenue, London W11 4QR

First published in Great Britain by Sinclair-Stevenson 1993
Paperback edition published by Granta Books 2004
This edition published by Granta Books 2012

A CIP catalogue record for this book
is available from the British Library.

1 3 5 7 9 10 8 6 4 2

ISBN 978 1 84708 632 7

Printed and bound by CPI Group (UK) Ltd, Croydon, CR0 4YY

MIX
Paper from
responsible sources
FSC® C020471

INTRODUCTION

Diana Athill published her first book, *Instead of a Letter*, in 1963. It starts conventionally enough, with an account of a 'middling English gentry' childhood of ponies, lawns and housemaids, offset by a lurch into poverty when servants had to be dispensed with, bar one 'to do the scrubbing and another to cook lunch'. At Oxford, aged nineteen, Athill got engaged to a bomber-pilot and made plans to join him in Egypt. 'I was going to ride a white Arab stallion and keep a white saluki to run behind me. We were going to have four children.' But the Second World War started and her fiancé's letters stopped. 'I never heard from him again until I received a formal note, two years later, asking me to release him from our engagement because he was about to marry someone else.' Soon afterwards, he was killed.

The second half of the book is an examination of what Athill calls 'the change brought about in my nature by my own loss of confidence'. She found she had to earn a living, and worked at the Admiralty and the BBC before helping to found a pair of publishing companies, Allan Wingate and André Deutsch. She had 'foolish and always short affairs', became pregnant and aborted the baby. 'Lack of energy prevented me from ranging about in pursuit of men, but if they turned up, I slept with them.' Her writing on sex is candid and instructive. Looking back on her adolescence, she wonders why she did not masturbate. 'If I had known of the activity I should certainly have indulged in it, but I did not know of it, and not having a strong practical bent, I did not invent it.'

Instead of a Letter is an eminently realistic feminist text, which has aged better than its contemporaries such as *The Golden Notebook* or *The L-Shaped Room*, with their weighty undertow of social polemic. Athill's perspective is unusual: she writes with the head but from the heart, questioning the friendly self-satisfaction of her class without mocking it, and shows how her upbringing both restricted and helped her in the changing Britain of the post-war years. It is astute, intuitive and hopeful; it is devoid of self-pity; it feels true. There is no reason to dispute a reviewer's suggestion that it should be 'pressed into the hands of every seventeen-year-old girl', just as Elizabeth David's *French Provincial Cooking* bears a quote saying, 'I would have a copy purchased by public funds and presented to every young wife on her wedding day.'

To write an honest memoir, without self-deception, is difficult, perhaps impossible. Athill comes close to it in her books. Reality liberates her in a way that fiction does not. Her 1967 novel, *Don't Look at Me Like That*, feels static compared to her various memoirs, despite being autobiographical. Jean Jacques Rousseau made a pioneering attempt at presenting the truth about himself in *The Confessions*, published shortly before the French Revolution. *'Je forme une entreprise qui n'eut jamais d'exemple . . .'*

'I have resolved upon an enterprise which has no precedent, and which, once complete, will have no imitator. My purpose is to display to my fellow-mortals a portrait in every way true to nature, and the man I shall portray will be myself.'

Others, like William Hazlitt in *Liber Amoris*, attempted to follow in Rousseau's footsteps, laying bare their misdeeds and mistakes, and trying to analyze their motivation, but were restricted by the law and by propriety.

During Athill's early days in publishing some subjects remained unmentionable. When Allan Wingate published Norman Mailer's *The Naked and the Dead* in 1949, the word 'fucking' had to be rendered – famously and ludicrously – as 'fugging', but still attracted the attention of the Attorney General. The editor of the *Sunday Times* condemned the book as so obscene that 'no decent man would leave it where his women or children might happen to see it.'

In 1968, five years after the publication of *Instead of a Letter*, an article appeared in the *Spectator* magazine decrying the developing climate of indiscretion. It was written in response to Michael Holroyd's biography of Lytton Strachey, which had broken ground by treating Strachey's homosexual affairs as a regular part of life. The piece suggested that public figures would now have to 'destroy their most intimate letters and be very careful what they write in their journals . . . So the private records of our times, perhaps the most articulate in history, will be paradoxically sparse unless we impose on ourselves some sort of limitation on what is to be published and when.' Five years on, the author of the article, Nigel Nicolson, produced *Portrait of a Marriage*, a frank account of the adventures of his bisexual parents, Harold Nicolson and Vita Sackville-West, and was in turn condemned for impropriety.

Today, only a generation later, social expectations have shifted. The internet leaks brutal pornography and reality television delights in extreme family dysfunction; it is beyond parody. No subject is taboo for a writer. A new kind of autobiographical writing has become popular, which at its best shows much about the way people live and think. The rise of the revelatory memoir is generally credited, in Britain at least, to books published in the early 1990s by writers such as Blake Morrison and Nick Hornby, but Diana Athill may have struck the first blow with *After a Funeral*.

Published in 1986, it examines her relationship with a young Egyptian writer during the 1960s, who later killed himself by taking an overdose of sleeping pills in her spare bedroom. She liked Didi – as she calls him in the book – from the moment he appeared at her house. He was charming, poor, attractive, displaced; and as Athill puts it, 'I was a sucker for oppressed foreigners.' She fell in love with him, despite being aware that Didi was not attracted to her physically. She arranged for him to get a visa, let him stay at her house and helped him to find employment. He soon went off in pursuit of other women. Typically, Athill offers an acute examination of her own motives. 'Sex and the maternal impulse are closely interwoven, particularly in childless women of middle age . . . I like being turned to and relied on, I like being seen as indulgent, understanding and reassuring – a motherly figure.'

Didi (the name an odd prefiguring of Dodi, another Diana's pet Egyptian) was a good cook and good company, but he was self-destructive and the arrangement quickly went wrong. Efforts to help him misfired. When given the chance to make some money by painting the house, 'he began carefully, but then decided that if he applied the whitewash very thickly, with rough strokes, it would give the walls an interesting texture.' Soon, the carpets were 'tracked with painty footprints'. They went on a disastrous holiday together, and afterwards Athill read Didi's diary and found cruel comments about herself. She asked him to leave; he had nowhere to go; they were reduced to communicating through notes left on the landing. One night, drunk, Didi got into bed with her. Athill's response was weirdly passive. Rather than telling him to go away – or leaping on him – she allowed him to have sex with her despite thinking, 'Tenderness would soon be counteracted by the weariness of my unaroused body, so I had better end this love-making by faking a climax and bringing Didi to his.'

It is this sort of detail that makes *After a Funeral* such an unusual and compelling book. Athill could easily have hidden the more foolish or unflattering aspects of her own behaviour, but did not. The *Washington Post* described it as one of the 'few totally honest accounts of a human life'. Behind the story of the relationship between one man and one woman lies a constant sense, stronger for being unvoiced, of Europe's colonial history and the uneasy relationship between ruler and ruled in the decades after the end of empire. Didi's impotent frustration at his protector's generous, industrious, rational, permissive English liberalism ends only with his death. As a record, and as a warning, *After a Funeral* is complemented by the crazier, but equally tragic, story that Athill tells here in *Make Believe*.

A good novelist will invent good names for her characters, but a writer who finds them in real life must be commended. The players in *Make Believe* include Al Donaldson, alias Hakim Abdullah Jamal, an African-American criminal turned hypnotic social activist, his English girlfriend-cum-slave Gale Ann Benson, alias Halé Kimga (an anagram of 'Hakim' and 'Gale') who was, inevitably, the daughter of a Tory MP (Captain Leonard Plugge, who claimed to have invented the two-way car radio), and Michael de Freitas, alias Michael X, alias Michael Abdul Malik. There is even a wealthy German dropout, 'deep in the process of discovering his own loathing of capitalism, violence, and racism, and the mind-expanding properties of cannabis', who has the perfectly Nabokovian name of Herbert G. Herbert.

Jamal was moved to change his life by the inspirational black American leader Malcolm X, a relation by marriage, of whom Malik was a pale imitation. While having an affair with the movie star Jean Seberg, Jamal met Vanessa Redgrave, who in the spirit of Sixties radicalism invited him to England to start a school. He was soon in the offices of André Deutsch, discussing books with Diana Athill. 'I sat down near him,' she writes, 'and within two minutes he had put his hand on my shoulder and was watching to see if I would flinch at being touched by this impertinent nigger.' She did not react. 'He must see that I was "different": the classic reaction of the white liberal on meeting a prickly black.' André Deutsch published Jamal's book, *From the Dead Level: Malcolm X and Me*, a racy account of his ghetto years in Roxbury, Boston, which reads like a prequel to the works of Quentin Tarantino: 'Niggers are a bitch . . . I'll cut your mother-fuckin' ass right here, you dig?' It carried a photograph of Jamal looking sexy and bad, with a period author's note:

> Hakim Jamal was born in Boston in 1931. Unlike many heroin addicts he always paid for his habit by working, not stealing, and has been a programme editor for a television magazine and a clerk in a legal office . . . He sees himself as fund-raiser, not teacher – indeed, refuses to teach for fear of teaching the children to hate. He is president of the Malcolm X Organisation of Afro-american Unity Inc, and a part-time member of the Black Panthers.

Full-time membership of the Black Panthers would have been a distraction for Jamal. His day was taken up with living off the land, finding white patrons, 'debating' them (which Athill describes as 'an exceptionally fatuous kind of verbal quibbling') and trying to promote his unstable, trans-formative fantasies. With Herbert G. Herbert, he made plans to found a utopian commune in Guyana.

Jamal had some coverage in the British press and appeared on BBC radio. He told Jill Tweedie in the *Guardian*: 'You should kill people because they are evil, not because they are white . . . They call me a nigger but I've invented my own kind of nigger. My nigger is me, excruciatingly hand-some, tantalizingly brown, fiercely articulate.' Tweedie was impressed. 'This black man is a handsome man', she wrote. His anger made her 'hopeful for the future'.

From time to time Jamal came to stay at Athill's house, and whether he was in a good, bad or disruptive mood, she found him 'impossible to disregard'. They took acid, talked and went to bed together, once. She was struck by 'some-thing which I suppose men to feel more often than women: the alarming power of beauty. It was a physical sensation, as though a floor under my heart had given way and it was about to drop into a gulf of excruciatingly intense longing for this magical creature.' We know from *After a Funeral* that

Athill is 'one of those people who are hardly ever totally involved in an emotion. There is almost always a "watcher" in the back of my mind, and a pretty beady-eyed watcher at that.' She has what Graham Greene called the 'splinter of ice' in the writer's heart. But still, even when Jamal told her he was God, the relationship continued.

'Everyone in this story was at some time or another at least a little mad', Athill wrote, and her act of lunacy was to offer Jamal a 'loan' of £200 so that he could return to the United States. He accepted on the condition that he might give her a weekend of loving, adding tactlessly that she should not think of herself as 'an old woman who is reduced to buying sex'. Athill was outraged, but invited him to stay all the same, this time accompanied by the unfortunate Gale Ann Benson who promptly stole the money out of a dressing-table drawer. They took over Athill's house, told her that she had vacated her body and taken possession of Benson's, and inveigled another £200 out of her. Throughout this bizarre and painful saga, Athill hoped that good manners would see her through; even when Jamal and Benson invaded her bedroom for compulsory debate, she found herself unable to tell them to get out. 'This was one of the occasions in my life – not many – when I've felt hamstrung by being "well brought up".' Finally, her guests decamped to Trinidad where they fell under the influence of Michael Abdul Malik, a rival messiah.

Malik was another André Deutsch author, although Athill believed from the start that he was a conman. His book was ghosted by Stephen John, the author of *Roman Orgy*. Malik was prone to turn up at her office 'ranting that he had secret information about concentration camps for blacks being built in Wales'. *From Michael de Freitas to Michael X* is the work of a pimp, thief and hustler who was promoted by the media as a black power leader and poet, with the encouragement of figures such as Alexander Trocchi, John Lennon and Yoko Ono. The final lines of the book read: 'The black man walking through the slums of Notting Hill says: "We should burn this fucking place down." You hear it every day. When the explosion does come it will be a very big one. And everyone will suffer. Black and white.'

Malik was in reality the son of a black Trinidadian woman and a Portuguese shop-keeper, who had come to London to seek his fortune through crime. As V. S. Naipaul wrote in his coruscating essay, *Michael X and the Black Power Killings in Trinidad*, 'He wasn't even black; he was "a fair-skin man", half white. That, in the Trinidad phrase, was the sweetest part of the joke.' Malik was taken up by Nigel Samuel, the young son of a rich property developer, and flown to Africa in a private plane 'to see the history and culture of the people we came from'. He founded the Black House in Islington and the Racial Adjustment Action Society, which, the *Observer* reported, had 45,000 members. The organization was in fact little more than its letterhead, an opportunity to cash in on political upheavals in the USA. 'American blacks are an excluded minority,' wrote Naipaul. 'West Indians come from countries with black majorities and black administrations.' Malik served time in prison for inciting racial hatred, suggested that the Queen should have a black baby and briefly became Minister of Defence for the Black Eagles, an outfit run by Darcus Howe, now better known as a flamboyant TV presenter. When his luck ran out, he returned to Trinidad and set up an agricultural commune. This was where Jamal and Benson arrived at the end of 1971.

No rivalry developed between Malik and Jamal. Instead, down on his luck, Jamal became entranced by Malik and accepted his demand that a human sacrifice was needed. Benson was hacked to death with a cutlass by Malik's associates and buried in a shallow grave. Unnerved, Jamal fled to Boston where he in turn was murdered by De Mau Mau, a militant organization established by black US soldiers in Vietnam. Malik was convicted and hanged in the Royal Gaol in the Port of Spain. His white patrons back in London refused to admit his guilt, despite powerful evidence against him. The countercultural ambassador John Michell produced a *Souvenir Programme for the Official Lynching of Michael Abdul Malik*, describing him as a 'gentle mystic' and 'architect of the Holy City'. Beneath a drawing of a white woman trying to have sex with the hanging corpse of a black man, Kate Millett was quoted: 'It's the hideous combination of racism and sexism that permits these kinds of trials to happen.'

Diana Athill ends *Make Believe* abruptly with the assertion that Hakim Jamal 'was a loving child unloved, a beautiful child made to believe he was ugly, a clever child starved into a process of desperate self-invention.' There is truth in this; his childhood was a familiar tale of deprivation and abandonment, but Athill's conclusion is sentimental. It accepts Jamal's belief that his fate was the responsibility of others. 'I gave school one more chance and it failed me,' is a typical line in *From the Dead Level*. Many African-Americans shared, and continue to share, Jamal's deprived upbringing, but they do not end up killing or being killed.

Athill's reputation as a writer has followed an unusual trajectory, boosted in her mid-eighties with the publication of *Stet*, her account of editing authors such as Naipaul, Molly Keane and Jean Rhys. It was followed in 2002 by *Yesterday Morning*, a relaxed, autumnal expansion of *Instead of a Letter*. Athill has enjoyed an Indian summer as a literary queen mother, popping up in newspapers and on the radio in the guise of a game old bird with a clipped, clear voice and a twinkle in her eye. The claim that she was one of the finest editors in British publishing is borne out by the André Deutsch archive, where her letters to authors are models of the detailed, perceptive, sensitive encouragement that keep a literary career going. The valedictory final lines of *Yesterday Morning* are more optimistic than anything in her earlier writing. She has beautiful memories of her childhood, and thinks, 'it is not entirely impossible that I might, like my mother, come to the end of my days murmuring about some random memory: "It was absolutely divine."'

I suspect that the 1960s were the toughest and most exciting years of Athill's life during which she learned things about herself and others that it would have been easier not to know. It was a decade of fantasy, idealism and deception, when people tried to right historical injustices in an often ludicrous way. Athill in the end, was not deceived, but she emerged from the decade with few illusions about human relations. Without that suffering, and the self-knowledge that came from it, we would not have had her finest books.

Diana Athill presents a precise version of herself in her writings. How do others see her? Jeremy Lewis, who worked at André Deutsch, describes Athill in his memoir of literary London, *Kindred Spirits*, as 'demure and self-effacing and arty in an unthreatening way'. In the office, Miss Athill was 'a modest, fresh-faced Englishwoman' who 'wore her grey hair in a bun' and 'beavered quietly in the background'.

One weekend, however, Lewis had to collect a key from Athill from a house in Ladbroke Grove.

From inside I could hear the pulse of pounding rock; no one answered – not surprisingly, given the pounding rock – so, feeling suitably unnerved, I tried again. Eventually the door was flung open by a black man wearing a tight black shirt, black jeans, wraparound dark glasses and a woolly hat like a tea-cosy, and wafting after him a sweet-smelling cloud of pot. By now I was certain I must have come to the wrong address – surely Diana must be elsewhere in Notting Hill, attending a meeting of PEN International or taking tea further along the Bayswater Road at the Royal Society of Literature? – but, having brought the man to the door and disrupted his afternoon, I felt I ought to ask. 'I'm terribly sorry to bother you,' I said, feeling unusually stiff and far from radical, 'but I'm looking for someone called Diana Athill, and I wondered . . .' At this he took me by the arm in the kindest and most unfrightening way and, urging me to make myself at home ('Come in, man, come and join the party'), ushered me into a large ground-floor room. The pounding rock was louder than ever, and the clouds of pot more Wagnerian: but as far as I could see – blinking uneasily across the jerking, gyrating bodies, and wondering what I should do were a joint to be thrust in my hand – there was no sign of Diana. I was just about to back away with more profuse apologies – he must have misheard me, or have had another Diana in mind – when a vaguely familiar-looking woman with long golden hair, clad in a shining yellow dress, came up to me, dangling a key in one hand, and said, in clear upper-class tones, 'Here's the key to the office, Jeremy – let me have it back in the morning, won't you?'

Returning the key on the Monday, seeing the grey bun, Lewis wondered if he had imagined the entire episode. Then he spotted 'hanging behind the door on a hook, a glittering golden wig'.*

Patrick French, June 2004

---

*On reading these lines, Diana Athill wrote to me: 'I never owned a "glittering golden wig" in all my life. At one time in the 60s I did buy in Selfridges one of their "fun wigs" – short brown curls – and it is just conceivable that I may have worn it to that party (I don't remember doing so) – but not that I'd have taken it to the office next morning!' I put this to Jeremy Lewis, who said he was certain that Diana had worn the wig, although he could not be sure of its precise colour, and he remembered seeing it in the office on the Monday. That was 'the crux of the story'. This illustrates another problem with the writing of a truthful memoir: memory is flexible. The biographer would ideally like an independent witness, a photograph, and a receipt specifying the putative wig's colour and provenance.

Make Believe

One

I liked Hakim Jamal at once. He was a dramatically handsome man, and his style – the piratical swagger, the single gold earring – pleased me because of what seemed an element of self-parody in it. The brightness of his eyes and the set of his mouth gave him an amused look as though his own act tickled him.

He had been invited to London in 1969 by people who thought he was doing interesting work organising progressive schools for black ghetto children in Los Angeles. His talk had convinced them that he ought to write a book and one of them had introduced him to an agent who brought him to André Deutsch publishers.

As soon as I came into the room Hakim stopped paying attention to the two men already there and focused on me. Unaccustomed to English people, he saw me as exotic and refined; my voice, he told me later, reminded him of Dame May Whitty (an actress who had played ladylike old Englishwomen in many films) and he said to himself that he'd better watch his language. I was a challenge. He was all set for the entertainment of seeing me recoil or bristle, or the satisfaction of seducing me (he particularly enjoyed being sexy to middle-aged women because it made him feel kind). I sat down near him – although I could have chosen a chair further away – and within two minutes he had put his hand on my shoulder and was watching to see if I would flinch at being touched by this impertinent nigger.

It was obviously a test and it amused me that he should be so wide of the mark. I didn't know many American blacks – none from such a violent ghetto background as I had been told his was – but I knew enough to expect them to be more jumpy about whites than my West Indian and African friends. I attributed the way Hakim came on to his background and felt him to be a challenge in my turn. He must see that I was 'different': the classic reaction of the white liberal on meeting a prickly black. I was wearing a wool dress but could feel the coldness of his hand on my shoulder through the material, and that it was trembling very slightly. I wanted to say, 'Relax, love – *I* don't have to be challenged or seduced, I'd be in bed with you in a trice if you wanted it.' A minute later he dropped a paper, bent to pick it up, brushed my knee with his hand and said: 'Oh look at me! I touched your knee by accident, I hope you don't mind.' It was hard to believe that such a confident-looking, handsome man could be so ridiculously tense and clumsy; that he could suppose that he was testing me in a wily fashion while making such a fool of himself. It struck me as both comic and touching.

Hakim had known Malcolm X when he was a boy and Malcolm was still a hustler, and had later been converted by him. He wanted to write a book about this. Keeping Malcolm's memory alive and spreading his teaching was, he said, by far the most important thing in his life because if he hadn't known Malcolm he'd have been dead in a gutter long ago. Yes, it was true that he had been both an alcoholic and a heroin addict until Malcolm got through to him; yes, it was true that he had kicked both addictions under the influence of Malcolm's teaching alone, without medical help, and many other people like him had done the same. No, he would not mind me editing his script if I thought it needed it – why should he, when he had never written anything before except a few short articles for minority magazines? Yes, he was prepared to write three trial chapters so that we could make up our minds, he'd let me have them in a couple of weeks.

A couple of weeks! One forgets, I thought, that people who know nothing about writing really know nothing. But he delivered his chapters when he said he would and they were direct and vivid stuff. The punctuation and grammar were shaky but the language was alive, with none of the stilted or grandiloquent straining after literary effects common in ill-educated writing. We signed the book up and from then on he was a model of punctuality, and of reasonableness without spinelessness when it came to discussing editorial suggestions. People were to say later that the Englishwoman he was living with, Gale Benson, wrote his book for him. She did not. No doubt she sometimes helped him over grammar or the meaning of a word (he never minded admitting ignorance of such things), but she did nothing more. The act of writing gave him great pleasure, and when it came to its essentials he considered himself Gale's teacher, not her pupil.

At the end of our first meeting I offered him my hand and he said, 'No no, my friends I kiss', and kissed me, both of us laughing. Weeks later I told him that he'd done that to needle the two white men present, but he said no, the kiss had been genuine because he'd already decided that he liked me. I accepted that as the truth, and was pleased.

He struck me at once as a man who had always had any woman he wanted, but not as a particularly sensual man: it would be seducing, not fucking, that was important to him. Probably he would be matter-of-fact about fucking, and I doubted whether he would ever care to find out much about a woman. He would be pleased and excited by the effect he was making on her, not the effect she was making on him. We had a couple of lunches together soon after our first meeting, before a break caused by my absence on a long holiday abroad, and at

3

both of them he bore down on me with all the charm he could muster. When he saw that I enjoyed it and made no resistance, he relaxed and each occasion became one of straightforward friendliness. I was slightly disappointed by this, but not surprised or hurt, having reached an age at which one can still hope for a flutter but has given up expecting it. I was fourteen years older than Hakim.

At one of these lunches he asked me to introduce him to a man called Michael Malik, whose original name was Michael de Freitas and who had recently dubbed himself Michael X and set up as a Black Power leader. He said he thought Michael might be able to help him, and when I asked how, he explained that even after ten years without heroin he still had spells of being twitchy, a kind of ghostly cold turkey (he gave me his hand to feel and it was icy, although the restaurant was warm). On these occasions it helped to be with someone familiar with drugs and their effects, and he supposed Michael would be such a man. I guessed that because Michael called himself X, Hakim hoped to find in him something of his hero Malcolm X, and I told him that he was wrong: Michael was no more Malcolm's heir than I was. 'You think he's phony too?' he said. 'Funny, other people have told me that, black as well as white. Maybe I'd better give him a miss.' I was glad of this, feeling that Michael would be more likely to steer someone back on to drugs than help him keep off them.

I didn't know Michael well, but disliked him. He had been introduced to André Deutsch several years earlier under impressive auspices as a newly discovered black leader who ought to be given a platform. I can claim witnesses to my saying, after one meeting, 'Let's leave him alone, he's either a nut or a conman'; but his patron carried weight and we were in a mood, as a firm, to be sympathetic to dissident voices, so it was agreed that if he could find a ghost writer we would consider his book. Later Michael was to talk, and probably to think, of himself as a writer, but then he made no secret of his near-illiteracy and even laughed at the idea that he might write the book himself. He was prepared to talk, but someone else must do the writing. His first candidate was incompetent, but then he found an Englishman who gave him a great deal of time and made a lively job of his story. Having gathered meanwhile that, whatever label he was given by whites, Michael was considered a joke by most blacks in England, I was relieved that the finished book seemed to be near enough to the facts to avoid making disproportionate claims for him. It showed how he saw himself politically, but also made it pretty clear how little his activity really amounted to. Its publication would not declare 'Here is the new Black Power Leader of Great Britain', but 'This is one kind of man turned out by a racist society'. Whether I liked Michael or not, I believed people should try to understand the processes that had formed people like him, so on balance I thought his autobiography worth doing.

There followed the most tiresome time we ever had with a book. On legal advice we asked for a few small alterations, to avoid the risk of libel suits. They made no difference to the book's message, being chiefly concerned with former girlfriends and cronies of Michael's, and he as well as us would be sued if anyone decided to take action, but he at once began to lie, saying that these people knew what he was saying and 'loved' it. We checked, and they didn't: all of them wanted alterations to be made and one of them stated flatly that she would sue if this wasn't done. At that point Michael began to make lunatic threats. If I pointed out that he only had to change a name or a date, he would answer by shouting that he was going to send his men to burn our office down, or would start ranting that he had secret information about concentration camps for blacks being built in Wales. After a two-hour session during which he accused me of surreptitiously changing his text, and replied to my suggestion that he take proofs and manuscript home and check them against each other at his leisure with more of his office-burning threats, I remember thinking, 'I wish they *were* building those concentration camps'.

The difference between my response to Michael and my response to Hakim was simply that I liked Hakim. He discussed his proposed book far more intelligently than Michael discussed his, and its subject matter was more interesting; but at bottom it was a matter of feeling warm towards him.

I had turned forty before I got to know any black person intimately, but when that happened, having unexpectedly found a lover who suited me perfectly and was to become an enduring friend, I began expecting to like blacks. A new white I would meet in neutrality, just waiting to see if I would like him or not; a new black I would meet with the positive expectation of enjoying his company against which he would have to prove himself uncongenial, if so he was…as Michael had done. In addition to this bent, which had come to seem like a natural one, I was also equipped by my age with a comfortable degree of security because I knew that I was proof against a certain kind of hurt. By that time, if a man could stir me sexually there was bound to be more pleasure in it than pain, however little came of it – the pleasure of feeling that my responses were not yet dead, that I was at least still capable of being reminded of the delicious emotional and physical sensations which used to be of such overwhelming importance in my life. With Hakim I could see that I would enjoy love-making if it happened, but if it didn't he would still be one of the oddest and most interesting people to find out about that I'd met for a long time. This ready but undemanding concentration on him of interest and sympathy was, I think, both soothing and stimulating to him, and was the reason why he found me easy to get on with.

He must have started living with Gale Benson – or, to give her the name he had bestowed on her, 'Halé Kimga' – just before we met, but he said nothing about her. He was staying with 'friends', about whom he used the pronoun 'they'. I assumed 'they' was a woman. He went on being secretive about her for some time. This reserve was not an attempt to appear unattached so that he could make love to other women. Rather it was because (I think) he felt that becoming seriously involved with a woman betrayed a shameful weakness, and his involvement with Halé was serious.

Another affair of his, which he could present as a piece of cold-blooded calculation, he described in detail at once, at our first lunch together. This was with a film star, Jean Seberg, and was important to him because it had abruptly – even violently – shifted the course of his career. It also had a good deal of straightforward snob value: he still felt it gratifying, though a little hard to believe, that *he* had hobnobbed with all the famous people in Jean's circle, and he didn't miss chances to let one know of it.

This affair, together with several hints about killing white people during the militant period of his Black Muslim allegiance, I stowed in a corner of my mind marked 'Query'. He might be fantasising. His commitment to making an effect caused him to look like a fantasiser. It was possible that he'd had an affair with this woman – handsome black men do get taken up by film actresses. It was possible that he had killed – a great many people, both white and black, get shot in the streets of American cities. But it was equally possible that he would simply have liked to have done these things. They made good listening, and I judged that sooner or later I would be able to tell if they were true or not, so I kept an open mind.

Hakim's chief credential was his part in founding the Malcolm X Montessori School in Los Angeles as a memorial to Malcolm. He had been invited to England to start another such school in London, or so he said. He did have a part in founding the Los Angeles school, and he had been its main fund-raiser, but by the time he reached England it had collapsed, and this he never told me or anyone else, although the way he talked about it did make me suspect that it no longer had much existence outside his head. He always came out with the same catch-phrases about it, and it seemed sadly likely that the little brochure he thrust on everyone was, by this time, all that was left of it. He was genuinely obsessed with the idea that black people should undertake their own education, and with the belief that education should start in earliest infancy; but he appeared to think that getting together a room, a teacher and a few kids was all that had to be done. He clearly had no inkling of the continuing problems involved in running a school. Once named, the thing was felt to exist... No, that is unfair, he took it a step further than that: the thing did have to be there, but it did not have to function. In London I saw him inspire two people – two penniless, cranky people with no experience of children, still less of teaching – to hang a sign above their door, give up one of their rooms to the children in their street, and devote all their spare time and energy to entertaining these children in ways as 'creative' as they could devise until, eighteen months later, one of them collapsed under the strain into a nervous breakdown. To Hakim this was 'starting a school in London'. To me it was a brave attempt that would evidently come to nothing. I

8

have heard people jibing at Hakim's 'so-called school' –
but what *can* happen when people with no money, no
pull, no suitable experience are driven to attempt the
solution of problems so immense and complex that so-
cieties pretend they don't exist? At best sketchy
improvisations, at worst fiasco; and if fiasco, then it
should be mourned, not mocked.

But I was less interested in the role Hakim claimed on
the black militant scene than in his personal story: the
way Malcolm's teaching had saved him from his addictions and altered his self-awareness. As a political figure
he was marginal, but he was a man to whom extraordinary things had happened because of his place in
society. To talk intimately with someone whose experience was so unlike my own was like reading some
fascinating book – but better, because I could question
and get answers.

He had at that time two ways of talking, rhetorical and
autobiographical. The rhetorical was dead boring. He
would rant with a crescendo of violence about white
guilt and his hatred of whites – stock stuff, for the most
part, playing on the white liberal's uneasiness; and also
a release of his own uneasiness into what he felt to be an
acceptable channel. It was often too compulsive to be a
deliberate ploy, and none of it was nonsense. The situation between blacks and whites *is* as he described it, and
there were moments when he was illuminating about
this. But too often he would be using it automatically, to
give himself the feeling that he had a raison d'être and
because he thought that it impressed people. I fell
quickly into the habit of letting this kind of talk flow by.
Sometimes I would go away and do something – perhaps make a pot of tea – until he was over it, and once
or twice I soothed him out of it by going behind his chair
and rubbing his shoulders, rocking him, saying, 'Cool it

love, I know, I know,' as though I were gentling a horse. He seemed quite grateful for being brought down to more concrete and interesting subjects.

And in his autobiographical vein he was concrete and interesting. Its tapping was a by-product of work on his book. Twice during the writing he came to stay in my flat, both times for about two weeks. I read what he had written – roughly the first half of the book the first time, the rest of it the second time – and made my comments, suggesting that he should expand this or explain that, and he carried out my suggestions, or produced alternatives of his own, during the day when I was at work. He was anxious not to put more about himself into the book than was necessary to explain the importance of Malcolm X's impact on him; it was Malcolm who mattered, he insisted, not himself. At first I thought that he was saying this only to make a good impression, but eventually I concluded that it was sincere. I often had to press him for more in the part of his book which deals with his life before he came under Malcolm's influence, and he was always reluctant to add more than a little. But these discussions brought details to his mind and he became increasingly absorbed in them, eager to talk about them even when he didn't want to include them in the book. We had talked enough for a whole extra book before we were through.

He went out very little during those weeks. When he had finished working on the book he would often do something useful such as peeling potatoes or washing the windows. It surprised me that he was such a tidy and considerate guest, and he himself was surprised by his considerateness though not by his tidiness; physical fastidiousness had obviously always been with him. I had a ragged, charred old pot-holder hanging by the stove and he always refused to touch it: 'That thing! Ugh – it looks like a malignant growth!' When I thanked him for something he'd done about the house he covered sheepishness by exclaiming with amusement at himself in a domesticated role. I was touched by his liking to help me in this way. Over supper we would gossip and laugh, and afterwards fall to talking about his life, sometimes until three in the morning, kissing each other an affectionate goodnight at the end of it and going to our separate beds. It was warm and easy – a very pleasant experience.

The easiness almost always vanished if anyone else was there, so I soon stopped having people round or suggesting that he should come with me to parties. With new people he would go at once into his swaggery, challenging act, usually more aggressively than he had done with me, and few were willing to ease him through it as I had done. They would become bored, angry, scared or embarrassed and he would react by becoming more boring, annoying, alarming or silly. He would plunge into what he called 'debating' people, by which he meant an exceptionally fatuous kind of verbal quibbling which would soon silence his opponent by its sheer pointlessness, whereupon he would interpret the other person's silence as his own triumph. He could produce a telling argument at times, but he seemed to value 'debating' more. Watching him make a fool of himself like this used to pain me, but I liked the relationship we had when he was relaxed too well to write him off. I preferred to think that he was 'himself' in that relationship, and to spare him those other times which rattled him into absurdity.

Most of his meetings with strangers ended in his abrupt departure. Afterwards he would say, 'I left because if I'd stayed in that room there'd have been a fight, and I didn't want to hurt him.' He told me of many such occasions, but he never did hit anyone, and the more violent he had been verbally, the more he was in a tremble about it. He could not resist inviting or provoking scenes, but was always distressed by them. He said that the main reason why he liked staying with me was because he needn't move about and meet new people and could have a rest from such upsets. On several occasions we discussed his provocativeness. He said he hated it, but however good his intentions were to start with, he was unable to check the impulse to tangle once it had started up. I learnt to spot it getting to work in him even before he entered a room.

Sometimes I saw him get through this disagreeable stage to a pleasant relationship, and what it demanded was a lot of genuine goodwill and honesty on the other person's part. I had quickly sensed that he had the neurotic's lightning instinct for detecting the real feelings of other people towards him, and knew that if I wanted to get on with him I must always tell him the truth. Several times I was to see him react savagely to social hypocrisy or the kind of pretence a white will put up to a black he feels he *ought* to be nice to; but he listened mildly to some highly unpleasant truths from me before we were through, such as that he was mad and suffering from delusions; that I wouldn't help him any more (he was on another book at the time) because he was writing nonsense; and that he couldn't stay with me again because he'd cost me too much in telephone calls to the States. About being mad he argued, but desperately rather than angrily. Until he went too deep into delusion to be reached except in terms of the delusion, he was something of a touchstone for kindness and honesty. I could tell in advance who would be able to take him: those who could genuinely start out as givers and who were more interested in being interested than in being interesting (the attention-hungry would have very lean pickings from Hakim).

After he had made a public exhibition of himself and had then made it worse, as he always did, by interpreting it as a triumph, it was a relief to find him intelligent and perceptive again as he was in his narrative mood.

In that mood his enjoyment of exact and pithy language became remarkable. He had a beautiful voice, and this combined with his feeling for words to make him an admirable raconteur. When we talked about people's behaviour or motives he was quick and sensitive. I told him once that he had a sense of style, and he said he didn't know what that meant. But he had it: at ease and enjoying himself, he always went straight to the telling detail in the right way, and if he used an odd or fanciful turn of phrase it was fresh and justified. The combination of this, his best way of talking, with the painful story of his childhood and youth was poignant.

Two

Hakim was born in 1933, long before the message that black is beautiful reached his native Roxbury – a black district of Boston. His mother walked out on the family when he was six; his father was a drunk and was not really his father (which pleased Hakim when he put two and two together later on, because he hated the man). Mother, her husband, his brother and sister were all light-skinned, particularly his mother who looked more like a Spanish woman than a Negro and was considered very beautiful. Hakim was told by his brother and sister that he was no kin of theirs: he had been found in the garbage pail and taken in out of kindness – let him look at the colour of his skin and he would see that this was true.

He saw that it was true and understood that he was ugly and inferior. Even his mother, whom he hungrily adored, had thought so because he could remember her saying when he was very little, 'At least you've got good hair' (this puzzled him later because his hair was like any other black person's). 'Poor little Al,' she used to say, rubbing his legs with Vaseline (when black skin is dry it shows up as a light grey powderiness). 'Al' because in those days his name was Alan Donaldson. As a small boy he supposed that they might throw him back into the street at any moment if he offended them. Still, at thirty-seven, he went into a panic if he accidentally broke something. When he broke a valueless tile in my flat he hid the pieces and it was three days before he could force himself to confess and explain the reason for the concealment: this humiliating panic, unamenable to any of the endless arguments he had with himself about it, legacy of that threat hanging over his childhood. 'Though God knows why I minded the thought of being thrown out,' he said, 'because I hated Blondie [his father] like hell. But I surely was dead scared all the same.'

When Blondie or a teacher at school heard other children jeering at him for being black, they turned on them in a furious, shocked way as though they had used a very filthy word. It was not the adults' attempt to protect him that stayed with him, but their disgust at 'blackness'. He couldn't help, he said, seeing his own arms and legs, but all through his childhood he tried to avoid seeing his own face in mirrors. If he didn't examine it he could go on hoping that it might be a bit less ugly and disgusting than he feared it was.

He started drinking at about ten, snitching capfuls of Blondie's liquor and topping up the bottles with water. By the age of twelve he was regularly getting drunk on wine – a chemical rot-gut, sold very cheap – and he shot his first heroin at fourteen.

At twelve he had found his mother again. He and the other two children had never stopped hoping she would come back, and he used regularly to lie if people asked whether the family had heard from her, pretending that they were in touch. He was always 'seeing' her in the street, his heart jumping, then going dead when it wasn't her after all. This time he'd gone to visit a friend who lived some way away from his own neighbourhood, and the friend's sister was the only person at home. 'Hi,' she said when she opened the door. 'What are you doing down this way? You visiting with your mother?'

He said he thought he would fall down but managed not to show it. But how was he to find out which house on this street his mother was in without betraying the fact that he hadn't known she was there? Looking back, he laughed at how obvious it must have been, but at the time he thought he'd managed it well: he said nonchalantly that he felt a fool because he never *could* remember which house was which in this street, they all looked so much the same. The girl teased him, but she pointed out the house: the one immediately across the road.

That posed another agonising problem. There were three apartments in the house, three bells at the door, and his friend's sister might be watching so he had to behave as though he knew which bell to ring. He chose the middle one and he was lucky. He didn't know the very big, very black man who answered the door, but the man recognised him and said, 'Have you come to see your mother? She's out, but come on in.' This was Smoothie, his mother's second husband who from then on was always kind to him and whom he came to love – the only person in his family he admitted loving. He hoped for a long time that Smoothie was his father, but when he asked him, many years later, Smoothie said, 'I wish that was so man, but it can't be. You was two years old when I started dating your mother.' (Later still he did identify his father, or thought he did, but it was a man he barely remembered and knew nothing about, so the knowledge was meaningless.)

Smoothie told him to come back next day when his mother would be in. Her first words to him were angry: what had he been doing the previous evening, out on the streets at that late hour? But he went back to her as often as she would let him, having instantly fallen in love with her. 'It wasn't any mother-son love, it was *being in love*. I remember one night sitting there watching her. She was lying on the sofa listening to the radio – there wasn't no TV in those days. She was so beautiful I wanted to kiss her in the *worst* way. I didn't want to fuck her – I knew about fucking by then, I'd had my first girl not long before. No, it wasn't that, it wasn't her body. It was her face, her mouth. It was so beautiful, so soft and gentle-looking. I was *dying* to kiss her. So when I was leaving I got up and crossed the room very quickly and I did kiss her – only a peck, I was too nervous. And she said "What's got into *you*?".'

She saw him as trouble even then, because although he sucked mints she could always detect the wine on his breath and she wanted nothing to do with another drunk. He bought her a present – a brooch in the shape of a red glass heart with gold filigree round it, which he thought very elegant at the time – but she never wore it.

In school he had done well to start with and was once described by a teacher as a brilliant child, but out of the first grade the teaching was poor and once the drinking started he was half asleep most of the time and he gave up.'They didn't like you asking questions, anyway. Before I gave up I was always getting slapped down.'

From school he went into the army – or from non-school, because towards the end he'd played hooky more often than he'd attended. At nineteen he was dishonourably discharged from the army for being a heroin addict. No treatment was given, he was simply tossed out, and within a year he'd been given a forty-year jail sentence for attempted murder and kidnap.

He'd been so drunk that he couldn't remember anything of what he'd done, but he was able to reconstitute it from the trial. He had quarrelled with a taxi-driver who was taking him to a station ('He'd insulted me for being black' he said, but for some reason that sounded like embroidery), had rammed a gun into the back of the man's neck and had forced him to drive out into the country. The taxi-driver had the presence of mind to switch on his radio contact with his base, so whatever was being said was overheard and the police had no trouble tracking the cab. Hakim felt sure that he could not in fact have been intending to kidnap the man although he might have meant to kill him, but it was the kidnapping charge that got him the very long sentence because they were in one of the Southern states where the law was particularly severe on this offence.

After serving four years of his sentence he was paroled. He never knew for sure how or why this had happened, but supposed that Smoothie, who was a well-respected man who had collaborated with white officialdom on some kind of community project, had contrived it.

I asked how painful the sudden withdrawal of heroin and alcohol had been, and he said that being frightened did much to take the mind off it, and that anyway there was always some substitute available. In that pen they had used nutmeg a lot. It was a bad drug, heavy and oppressive, but strong. 'Nutmeg?' I asked. 'The spice used in cooking?' And he said yes, you chewed it. I had forgotten at the time that Malcolm X, in his autobiography, describes the use of nutmeg in prisons in much the same way; only on rereading Malcolm's book some time later did I wonder if Hakim had 'borrowed' this detail from his hero. But none of the rest of his prison talk is in Malcolm's book.

He was frightened every day he was in the pen, first of rats, second of being raped. There was never a night when he didn't wake up with rats running over his bunk, and he had an intense horror of them; and the old lags used to creep into a man's bunk, press a razor-blade against his throat and say 'Do you want my prick in your ass or my blade in your throat?'

It was a Southern penitentiary. He might have worked with a mule team, but being a city boy he knew nothing about animals and was so terrified of the mules that he couldn't make himself go into a stall with one of them (I was surprised at how readily he admitted to being frightened). 'They kept telling me it was a good job, but after a bit they saw I'd rather be beaten to death than touch one of those things, so from then on I was grubbing stumps – that was all the work I did, grubbed stumps.'*

Soon after Hakim (or Al, as he was still called) was paroled, he made another drunken attempt to kill a man.

*Grubbing stumps – clearing land, hacking out the roots of trees with a pickaxe.

They told him he tried to cut the man's throat by sawing it back and forth on the glass of a car window (he found this interesting: it wasn't a way of killing which would normally have occurred to him, and there was something speculative in his tone when he spoke of it, as though he were trying to remember what it had felt like). This time they sent him to the nut-house, not to jail. It had hung in the balance, he said; it was only because the police doctor happened to find him interesting that the balance tipped that way. Other people considered it a disgrace to be in the nut-house, while they took jail for granted as something which happened to nearly everyone sooner or later, but he had never felt too bad about it because he had such a good time there. One of the doctors took him under his wing and for the first time he discovered the pleasure of probing his own behaviour, having been assured that he wasn't mad, but only someone who had more emotional problems to cope with than he knew how to manage. He drank a great deal, stealing surgical alcohol and mixing it with Coke, 'But I never had one bad drink all the time I was in that place, only happy ones.' It was clear that he genuinely remembered it as a safe and pleasant time; but his reaction to the fact that it ended because 'his' doctor was killed in a fire was chilling. No word about the doctor; only, 'Now wasn't that just my luck!'

He had a lot of women both before and after he married Dorothy (his mother was called Dorothy too) whom he treated abominably by his own account. Many years later she was to say in a letter 'You weren't really all that bad', but her expectations had probably been low. He must have been less sodden than he saw himself on looking back, because he'd had the sense to take advantage of a training scheme for ex-army men and had qualified as a linotype operator, becoming proud of being a good one. I suspect – although he was cagy about this – that he made money as a pusher as well as by working at his job, but he did work, and Dorothy stayed with him and was able to feed the children (they had six eventually, but three were born in better times, after his cure). He was always as thin as a whip but was physically very strong, and seems to have been able to stand up to his addictions better than most. His drug-taking friends tended to pay for their habits by stealing, but he agreed with Smoothie who had told him 'Never go in for that game unless you're going to do it professionally – it's too much of a risk.'

Then, when he was twenty-six, he had his first experience of the Black Muslims and of Malcolm X as a preacher. At twenty-seven he was converted, and from then on, for ten years by the time I met him, never another drink or another needle; and, whatever the objective facts of his behaviour, from then on the subjective feeling that his life had a purpose, that of making his black brothers see that they must become independent of whites and turn themselves into people who could be proud. He has described all this himself, in his book *From the Dead Level*, so I won't enlarge on it except to note one thing.

To Hakim his personal acquaintance with Malcolm X, and the fact that Malcolm was a distant cousin of Dorothy's, was of vast importance. He presented himself as 'Malcolm X's cousin', emphasised a slight likeness to Malcolm by wearing the same sort of hat and glasses, and based his claim to be listened to on his having *known* Malcolm. The acquaintance was in fact slight, and the times he had been with Malcolm as distinct from listening to his preaching in a Muslim temple were few. Once, shortly before his death, Malcolm did ask him to do something for him, but this incident, climactic in Hakim's eyes, must have been comparatively unimportant in Malcolm's, since nothing much happened. It is not surprising, therefore, that people have described Hakim as a fraud who was inventing a relationship with Malcolm in order to advance himself.

Against this: how do I know the gap between the importance this connection had in his eyes and its real nature? From *his own account* of it. It was he who told me that Malcolm's distant family relationship was with Dorothy, not him, and he who chose to make the fact public in his book, emphasising it in his dedication to Dorothy 'For holding on to me when all the lights went out…and for making Malcolm X my cousin'. And it was his own written accounts of his few personal encounters with Malcolm which made their triviality clear. These are scrupulous. He took pains not to distort them. Not once did he try to 'blow up' the facts on which he was basing his own claims to attention. What he did was odder: he attributed great importance to small facts, like a man handing you some object weighing only a few ounces and saying in all sincerity, 'Feel how heavy this is!'

I was disappointed by the second half of his book, to him the most valuable part because it was about Malcolm's preaching. It disappointed me because of the slightness of the facts and the naiveté of the interpretations. I made some attempt to steer him into a more sophisticated treatment, but gave it up when he was reluctant to play, and I realised that if I overcame his reluctance it would no longer be genuinely his book. How could it not have been naive? When hungry sheep have looked up and not been fed for a long time, they will fall ravenously on any weed. From *Malcolm X Speaks* I conclude that he was in fact offering them genuine fodder, but the way they fell on it was the way they would have fallen on anything, good or bad, wholesome or poisonous; and it seems to me now that Hakim, in demonstrating that way, was giving a more accurate picture than he knew of the impact of Black Muslim teaching, and of Malcolm, on the ghettos of his day.

*

This way of exaggerating the value of things that had happened to him seems to me to indicate the reason why Hakim did not usually lie. Almost all the stories I'd kept in my mind with a query against them were eventually brought out and labelled 'true', for the reason that so many of his most unlikely-sounding tales were substantiated. The affair with Jean Seberg was confirmed by Jean Seberg; his picture of his childhood and youth was confirmed in general, and in many specific details, by a friend of his called Charles Gooding who had grown up with him; and the more public events of his life – prison sentences, embroilments with the police, collaboration with the Panthers, an attack on the building which housed his school – were substantiated by press cuttings. Before his last visit to England he and Halé spent almost a year in the United States and Halé made it her business to collect documentation of his life. Describing herself as a newspaper reporter she visited police stations in places where he had lived, and she spent hours in public libraries with files of newspapers. She made photostats of what she found and kept them in scrapbooks dedicated to Hakim and his works, which she showed me. The police, I gathered, had annoyed her by tending to be dismissive about him, but there were a surprising number of cuttings. I had, for example, doubted the forty-year prison sentence because there was such a discrepancy between a sentence that long and getting parole after four years: I thought he might be piling it on to make it more dramatic. But there it was, a little item tucked away at the foot of a column.

The only stories which were not confirmed were those about going out to shoot, and actually shooting, white people in the streets during the early stages of his adherence to the Black Muslims. He said that for a time it was their policy to respond to any outrage against a black by picking off a white at random, and that he had done this several times. Either he had, without ever being suspected, or he had not, and lied in order to appear more excitingly dangerous than he was. Given the way he always escaped – and escaped in a state of great nervous agitation – from the consequences of his own provocative behaviour, I have concluded that Hakim had a lot of nervousness to contend with and might well have been inventing these murders in an attempt to seem as bold as he wanted to be. But that is no more than a guess made at the time of writing. When I was looking at Halé's scrapbooks I did not even remember his tales of race-war murders, having – I suppose – simply chosen to disbelieve them and consign them to oblivion because only on one occasion did he ever frighten me, and that in a way that had nothing to do with race.

The scrapbooks' confirmation of other matters did not surprise me, because by then I had become persuaded by his consistency. The events of his life and the caste of characters in it were the same whenever they reappeared and whomever they were produced for. This did not mean that Hakim never lied – I was sure he would have no scruples about doing so if he felt it necessary – but I reckoned that he usually found the truth so fascinating that he couldn't resist it. To such an egocentric man even the trivial was portentous if it affected him, so he would feel little need to make himself appear more interesting by distorting or magnifying what had happened to him. (The murder stories *might* have been an exception to this because they related to his standing as a militant.) Usually, if the way something had been didn't suit him he would deal with it by keeping silent about it (as he did over the collapse of the school), or sometimes by misremembering it; but that, which seemed to relate only to a certain kind of incident and to be a symptom of derangement, I didn't observe till later. Otherwise, apart from a few small lies of convenience which he hardly bothered to make convincing,

I had come to think that what he said could be believed.

The story of that beautiful child being made to hate and despise himself wrung my heart, and the extent to which he had been stunted and twisted by his circumstances enraged me. Once, when I told a white man about the child's belief that he'd been found in a garbage pail, the man said dismissively, 'Oh that – that's a chestnut of black childhood.' I had heard Hakim tell it, and had also seen a letter from his sister, written years later, asking him to forgive her because she had known no better. Looking at the white man, I felt hatred. If it was indeed a 'chestnut' had he not asked himself how and why it became one? He was resenting the demand such a story makes on sympathy. Had it not occurred to him that people with such stories to tell don't exist simply for the tiresome purpose of making him feel uncomfortable, but have lived what they tell with flesh, bones, nerves, brains as real as his own? You mean-souled, grey-blooded bastard! I thought, and still do.

My emotional response to Hakim is summed up by the following incident. He had said, 'I am not very good at reading' and I'd taken him to mean that he didn't care for it; and a little later he had said of an article by Camus in an old *Evergreen*, 'Now there's a writer I like' and I'd taken him to be pretending. Then one night I put my head round the sitting-room door, moving quietly, to tell him that the bathroom was free, and he was sitting there reading the Camus article, his brows knitted, his lips moving, following the line with his finger, and I saw with a shock that he'd meant 'not very good' quite literally. This man who loved words so much, who could rattle them down on to paper as fast as his typewriter could go (almost always spelling them right, which seemed extraordinary but was perhaps the result of his typesetter's experience), had done so little reading that he was reduced to spelling a book out like a child. I crept away and at that moment what I felt would have to be called love. Having my heart wrung is a sure way of inducing the sensations of love.

When Hakim was talking about his past he didn't appear to be trying to win the listener's sympathy. I once came across a quotation from a psychologist – I can't remember who, or where it was – saying that a common feature in psychopaths is an uncanny ability to sense and provide exactly what the analyst who is treating them wants to hear. Perhaps I, at that time, was in a relationship with Hakim not unlike that of analyst and patient. It may have been in response to my enjoyment of 'getting things right' that he adopted that attitude towards his memories, and to feed my weakness for having my heart wrung that he poured out his story so freely. But against that he was, as I have said, a man fascinated by himself. I felt it to be more likely that he was 'autobiographing' with such intensity more for his own satisfaction than to get a response from me, although my response probably added to his satisfaction. Several times he said that he was telling me things he had told no one else. This was not true: he had told Halé everything he told me. But it is possible that she and I were the people to whom he told most, because she and I both, at that time, made him feel safe and important. It seemed as though it were that which got him going rather than a desire to impress...or perhaps I should say rather than an unmixed desire to impress, since that desire was as constant a part of Hakim's personality as his digestion was of his bodily functions.

But he did strikingly exemplify another point made by that same psychologist: that psychopaths often exert great magnetism. A man who knew Hakim well once told me, 'I'm always disappointed when I read something by him – it's so much more convincing when he talks it', and on women it worked even more strongly. If Hakim came to stand by my chair and was 'giving it off' at me (deliberately? I was not always sure), I was always amused to notice the effort I had to make not to lean towards him; and twice I found it impossible to get up and leave the room, or even to take my eyes off his face, although I was resenting what he was saying as disagreeable nonsense. Halé he could hypnotise in the strict sense of the word, playing that old hypnotist's trick of making her bridge the space between two chairs, head on one and heels on the other. In a sweet mood he could establish a feeling of harmony and peacefulness (I know that Halé, Jean Seberg and two other women all remembered such occasions as precious, and I enjoyed some of them myself). In an evil mood he could harass and exhaust one, however little whatever he was up to mattered to one in any serious way. I have never known anyone so impossible to disregard.

Three

At the time of Hakim's two stays in my flat there was, of course, a sexual undercurrent to our friendship. It was less one of desire than of tenderness. From time to time as we talked he would wander over to me and give me a gentle, absent-minded kiss; or I would stroke his cheek as I passed his chair (his cheekbones, temples and the bridge of his nose were modelled with exceptional delicacy, agreeable to touch). These caresses were given with an odd sort of attentive gravity, yet at the same time 'in passing'. They were pleasing but not sexually arousing in the limited, physical sense.

On his first stay he told me that since he had gone to live in Agadir several months earlier he had been 'entirely celibate'. I never supposed that this was even *meant* to be believed, interpreting it as a courteous way out of having to make love to me, which he couldn't have been wanting to do or he'd have done it. I was not surprised, therefore, at the speed with which he fell on two pretty young girls who came his way during this so-called celibate time, one of whom offered herself to him as on a dish garnished with mayonnaise and whose infatuation obviously had to be, and was, rewarded; and the other who set herself against him in argument and obviously had to be, and was, brought to heel. To the second he was in some way disagreeable in bed; I don't know how, but she said to me afterwards, 'He's a bit kinky about sex, isn't he?'

The way we finally went to bed together affected my attitude to him a good deal. At the end of his first visit to my flat he was leaving for the US to collect (so he said) some tapes he needed in connection with his book, and he was dreading it – really very frightened. (And he was indeed arrested on arrival at Kennedy because a friend meeting him was seen slipping a gun into his pocket. Hakim was kept in the Tombs for a week pending trial – a noisome experience – and was given a suspended sentence.) On his last evening with me he was painfully tense, trying to talk himself through his fear, reminding himself that he was always frightened *before* but never *while* things happened, so if he wasn't going to be scared when something went wrong (if it did), how foolish to be scared now, when all was well. He was in for a sleepless night, he said – or perhaps not, if he took a couple of tranquillisers. He hadn't been using them for some days (he had depended on them a lot since he kicked heroin) but he needed them now. I went to have a bath and thought while in it that I could make him sleep if he came to bed with me. When I came out he was crossing the hall to his bedroom. I stood in the doorway to say goodnight while he knelt by his suitcase, digging about for the bottle of capsules. He looked miserable and his hands were shaking. So I said, 'Love, when you're in a nervous state like this is it easier to sleep alone or with someone? Because if you'd like to come and snuggle up with me you're welcome.' He answered, 'I may well do just that,' and after he'd cleaned his teeth he came into my room and undressed and got into bed as naturally as though we were an old married couple.

We lay on our backs holding hands, each waiting for the other to make the first move, but not tensely. Then I shifted my head so that my cheek was against his shoulder, and he turned his and kissed me. The love-making which followed was, as I had expected, straightforward and not especially exciting or excited. I had supposed that because of his beautiful proportions he would be delicious to hold, but he was too thin – his skinniness felt sad under my hands.

It was afterwards that the real love-making began, taking me by surprise. It was as though he sank right into me with the release of tension. He lay on me, holding me, kissing and kissing and kissing my cheeks, my eyes and my mouth, over and over again. For more than half an hour we lay like that while he ceaselessly and lovingly kissed me and I, from time to time, kissed him. The fucking hadn't made me come, but the tenderness of this did, very sweetly. We were both totally relaxed and went to sleep like that, almost blended into one, sweat feeling silky and pleasant, not oppressive. He didn't say much except, sleepily, 'I should have done this long ago,' and 'This isn't good fucking, it's good love-making.' It would be inaccurate to call it anything less than a beautiful night.

Once he raised his head to look down on me and I opened my eyes. It was not very dark so I could see him fairly clearly, and the shape and poise of his head and the grave tenderness of his expression made me shut my eyes again quickly. For an instant I had felt piercingly something which I suppose men to feel more often than women: the alarming power of beauty. It was a physical sensation, as though a floor under my heart had given way and it was about to drop into a gulf of excruciatingly intense longing for this magical creature. Once my eyelids shut the image out, the feeling stopped. Afterwards I was pleased that I'd had it, but even more pleased that it had only lasted a few seconds: how appalling to be lastingly the victim of such a feeling simply because of how someone looked! I also thought afterwards that incest must be delicious, because it seemed very much that it was my motherliness he was embracing so tenderly, and that I was exercising with so much pleasure in return.

Next day we said an affectionate farewell and I lay awake for a time that night, worrying about how his arrival in the States had gone. Three days later I learnt by chance that he had not in fact arrived there for another twenty-four hours, but had stayed another night in London, sleeping on the floor of a bedsitter in Kilburn. Had he missed his plane? Had he always meant to stay on? Had he not telephoned me because he felt it would be unartistic to spoil such a nicely judged parting, or because he'd put me out of his mind? Salutory questions to be left with, I decided; reminders that it would never do to start expecting anything from Hakim. I must stay on my own path while he followed his, and the only 'relationship' there could ever be between us would be the occasional intersection of those paths.

We slept together only twice more in all our acquaintance (both times it was enjoyable), but this slight sexual affair made me feel even warmer towards him so that his eventual 'impossibility' was all the sadder. In my experience the degree of physical tenderness expressed between us that night is uncommon, and I wanted it to – felt it *ought* to – represent a real closeness.

There was one love-making which failed to happen, after having been carefully planned by him to provide me with a transcendental experience. It was on the last day of his second visit, when he arranged for us to take an LSD trip together. He had recently taken his first and had been enchanted by it. His description of the pure delight he had experienced – the visual beauty of everything, its amusingness, its interest, the feeling of innocent vitality which had possessed him, the release he'd found in fits of absurd laughter – was so vivid that I was eager to join him. He was confident that he could control our joint trip and make it beautiful for both of us, and although I knew that trips don't necessarily resemble each other either from one time to another, or from one person to another, and that it's risky to go on one without the presence of a sober guide, I decided that given our joint goodwill it was a fair bet that this one would work. Hakim didn't say in so many words that its climax would be another beautiful love-making, but he intended it to be so, and I knew it.

Unfortunately the stuff he procured must have been adulterated. It was not, I think, a 'bad trip' in the usual sense, because the 'badness' was merely a matter of feeling physically ill and we both felt ill in the same way. After an hour or so of the usual pleasures – colours glowing, shapes changing in amusing ways or acquiring a fascinating significance (a sea-shell; a red rose which we scattered with water-drops which became star-like) – we began to feel sick. At no time did I seriously think I was going to throw up, but for the rest of the trip I knew I must keep still, keep quiet, keep my mind empty, just let time pass, or the diffused feeling of nausea would concentrate with horrible consequences. Hakim felt exactly the same. At one point the telephone rang and I answered it. I was able to speak normally, but when I flopped back into my chair I felt so bad that I doubted if I could make it to the lavatory, supposing that the exertion was going to bring me to vomiting-point. And soon afterwards a particularly boring hanger-on of Hakim's walked into the room. The children downstairs must have left the front door open, but at the time his sudden appearance seemed uncanny. Hakim pulled himself together and began to make polite conversation – the man wanted, for some reason, to talk about his car – but I, after one or two attempts, knew I wasn't up to it. I looked at the man and saw that he was undoubtedly mad; and understood that if I had to go on attending to him I might well be into a genuinely bad trip, not just feeling ill but seeing frightening things. I couldn't think why Hakim was being so attentive and kind. Why didn't he make the man go away? Finally I couldn't bear it any more. Taking care to speak as courteously as possible, I said that I wasn't feeling well and must go to my bedroom to lie down for a while. At this Hakim got to his feet, said to the man, 'Come on, I'll come and have a look at this car of yours,' and they went out. I tried to believe that Hakim was getting rid of him, but I knew before I heard the front door slam that he'd gone off with him and wasn't going to come back.

For a while I lay in my chair feeling forlorn at being abandoned, then I started to feel frightened. Supposing this trip turned really bad, what would happen to me now that I was alone? With a painful effort I forced myself to get up and go downstairs to tell my neighbours in the flat below what had happened, so that they could look in on me from time to time – which they kindly and comfortingly did. After that it was simply a matter of waiting, telling myself that the effects of this bloody pill were bound to wear off sooner or later. I couldn't take much interest in the strange things which happened when I opened my eyes – the chair which swelled to twice its size and started to breathe, the way the room changed shape, sometimes existing almost entirely in terms of its horizontal lines, sometimes in terms of its vertical lines. These events were no more than indications that I still had quite a time to go. I was worried about Hakim. He was supposed to leave for the airport early next morning. Would he come back in time? Would he collapse? I was sure that I would collapse if I had to move about, and he would be feeling just as ill as I was. But I realised that if I dwelt on worry it might swell to alarming proportions under the influence of the drug, so I told myself firmly that Hakim was capable of looking after himself, and closed my mind to the subject. Some time during the night it seemed worth going to bed but I still couldn't sleep. I lay inert, letting the night sounds and my bodily sensations absorb me.

We had taken the drug at three-thirty in the afternoon. By five-thirty next morning, when I heard Hakim come in, I was still feeling odd but was able to get up. I found him standing in the sitting-room, staring into the fire, and told him how glad I was that he was safely back.

What had happened? He said that he'd gone through an appalling night. He had never felt so nauseated in his life, he didn't know how he had dragged himself through it, tinkering with that fucking car for John and then being made to eat fish and chips, which had nearly done for him. No, he didn't think John had twigged. The reason he hadn't been able to get away was that the effort would have been beyond him.

I asked him why he'd gone off. There had been moments during the night when I'd felt stricken by his departure, but by now I knew that there was no telling how the pill would act. 'It was when you didn't make John go away,' he said. 'You wanted to go to your room and I thought you were rejecting me.'

'Oh *darling*!' I said. 'How daft can you get! I was desperate because *you* weren't getting rid of him!' By now I was able to find this misunderstanding funny, but Hakim, because of the ridiculous night he had spent, was further from recovery than I was and went on being stubbornly gloomy, so I sat him down and went to make him tea. Neither of us could drink more than a mouthful of it. Whatever that pill was, it was strong. I had no inclination to eat, drink, smoke or sleep for thirty-six hours after taking it (though all I felt when its effects wore off was a pleasurably normal degree of readiness to eat and sleep).

'I was going to make love to you,' he said miserably.

'I know, love,' I said, 'but never mind, it doesn't matter,' and I sat on the floor beside him, holding his hand. I felt fond of him for his childish disappointment at the failure of his plan. Then he turned my face up towards him, fixed my eyes with his, and began gently but forcefully telling me good things about myself: that I was his idea of a perfect woman, gentle and kind and good and beautiful and intelligent; that I mustn't feel sad about getting old because I was still all those things; that I must be happy and serene because he loved me. I was deeply moved. It was apparent to me that he was not expressing his feelings about me so much as *making me a present* (as he would have been doing if he'd made love to me). He was 'rewarding' me, 'bestowing' something on me in token of his favour. There was, in other words, no real meaning in what he was saying, but the impulse was a benevolent and generous one, and it was touching that he should overcome his exhaustion and physical malaise in order to express it so handsomely. He's as mad as a coot, I thought (because, as I shall soon explain, I had begun to notice symptoms by then), but it's a kind and loving madness, bless him. We parted that time with even more tenderness than the time before; and he, poor man, had an atrocious flight back to Morocco, feeling indescribably ill all the way.

Four

The third time Hakim turned up Halé was with him. She had gradually been allowed out of the shadows. First there had been references to 'a friend of mine' in Agadir who was studying to be a photographer, then this friend had become 'she', then there had been re- marks suggesting that he and 'she' were together quite often. After that I started asking questions about her *as though he had told me* she was his resident woman, whereupon he was suddenly eager to talk about their relationship and it became apparent that they had been having a very good time together and were both so happy in Morocco that they dreaded having to move on.

But before describing Halé I should note what evi- dence of madness there had been up to then, during a period of about a year which had included a good deal of correspondence, four or five short meetings in the first few months, and his two stays in my flat.

Before the first stay, about the fourth time he tele- phoned me, his call took me by surprise and I thought at first he was someone else. 'How come you didn't know it was me?' he asked. I asked why I should, and he said 'How could you fail to expect a call from God?' He said it as though he were joking and I took it as a joke – it only stuck in my mind because I was struck by its silliness as such. Early in his first stay, when I was admiring something he had done, he said, 'But then you must remember that I am God.' Again the tone was facetious, as it was when occasionally he made other big claims like, 'Haven't you realised yet that I'm never wrong?' or 'Of course I'm a genius'. When he made what

I took to be the God jokes I thought he was parodying his own tendency to boast, and he appeared to assent to my interpretation. I thought it a childish form of humour, but he didn't indulge in it often enough to be boring.

On the second visit, near the beginning, he made a similar remark which I have forgotten, then followed it a little later (we were in the kitchen and he was drying a plate) by giving me a grave look and saying 'You *really* don't believe I'm God, do you?' That I remember clearly, because it was the first time it occurred to me that he might mean what he said. I answered that of course I didn't, he was silent for a while, then he reverted to normal talk and that was that.

From then on the God jokes fell into place with other things, and I knew that I must take into account the possibility that he might be subject to fits of paranoia. I asked myself whether he just had moments of feeling that he was God, or did he feel it all the time but manage to keep it hidden except for these moments? On the whole the first explanation seemed the more likely. He gave the impression, always, of being wholly committed to the present, involved with exceptional intensity in what he was saying or doing, and for so much of our time together he was obviously not being God; besides which, of course, I *wanted* him not to be God. So my conclusion was that the balance of his sanity was rocky, but that it wouldn't necessarily tip.

The things with which the God jokes tied in were two. First, on several occasions his rhetorical fits had run on into wild talk betraying a distinctly dotty interest in the occult. In these moods he would refer in a more or less veiled way to the Masons, showing himself to be fascinated by the idea of mysterious powers stemming from esoteric knowledge. He knew a good deal of Masonic claptrap and would describe it half as though inviting me to mock at it, but seeming at the same time on the edge of skidding into credulity. I had met other people, dotty rather than downright mad, who loved to be credulous about such things, and I thought it a pity that this obviously excitable man must have come across such people and been influenced by them. When I tried to argue with him in these moods I found that I could only make an impression by taking him up at his own level, using parables and metaphor, and because I wanted to respect him I disliked 'handling' him in this way. So mostly I ignored these aberrations until they 'went away', which they did soon enough, and I had (or seemed to have) a rational man to deal with again. During both his visits to me these signs of dottiness went off as the days passed, and my vanity was flattered by the thought that I had a soothing and stabilising effect on him. (Towards the end of the second visit it occurred to me that I could now risk going to the theatre with him, and sure enough he made no attempt to tangle with strangers or to impress the people sitting near him, but enjoyed the play and behaved calmly and normally from beginning to end.)

The second warning sign was his description of a breakdown he had suffered about a year before we met. He was under great strain at the time because of his affair with Jean Seberg. When he met her he was ranking high in his own group as a militant anti-white. He had already broken with the Muslims in favour of the less extreme, more intelligent Malcolm X, but was not, it seems, paying much attention to Malcolm's thinking since he was still using Muslim terminology and insisting that all whites were literally devils. Jean picked him up on a flight back to Los Angeles from some place where he'd been giving a fund-raising talk (she was already interested in the black cause, and that cause had produced few conspicuous figures as handsome as Hakim) and he responded in a natural way. Here was a glamorous woman offering herself, and it didn't take him long to get over his incredulity and accept the chance. He was acting simultaneously as the old Al, who would obviously score such a woman if he could and was tickled by the whole set up of grand houses, private jet-planes and famous people, and as the new Hakim Jamal whose school had just been burnt down (no one knew by whom) and who was desperate to raise money for its rebuilding. 'Al' needed no urging; 'Hakim' was ready to go into a panic of guilt until one of his friends, hearing that he had met a film star, said 'Come *on*, boy, we can use your dick.'

On that suggestion Hakim pounced. Of course he had no business in bed with a white woman if he went there for pleasure, but if it was a duty...Malcolm X had said that the fight for equality and dignity must be carried on 'by any means necessary'. All right, the school did have to have money, didn't it?

Jean Seberg was compulsively generous with money, and also (which he told me with far greater admiration) with her time and energy. She really went to work for the school, contributing a lot of money herself and whipping up more from her friends. She also organised, or tried to organise, a relay of 'names' to sleep in the school building at night, after another bombing had been threatened, so that it couldn't be damaged without great scandal. And Hakim said to his friends, to his wife, and even more emphatically to himself: 'None of this would have happened if I hadn't fucked the dame. Don't think I *want* to do it. She doesn't send me, I can't even come with her [surely an invitation to disbelief? But that's what he told me he said]. I'm doing it for the sake of the school because Malcolm told us BY ANY MEANS NECESSARY.' And when he told me how he had said all this to his friends he was not distancing himself from the argument, but repeating it.

Whereas in fact he and this woman had been having an exciting time together and it's my belief that he was nearer to being in love than he had ever been before.

I first guessed at this from his over-insistent way of putting his version across. Then, as he relaxed, his references to things they had done together, to things she had said, to aspects of her personality and so on made it even clearer. She was the best-informed and most sophisticated woman he had ever met, and he loved talking to her. They had a good time in bed, too – though he was slightly shocked (I learnt this later) when she introduced him to a habit fashionable in her circle at that time: sniffing a capsule of amyl nitrate at the moment of orgasm, which has, it seems, a stunning effect. Final confirmation came from her letters to him.

Hakim carried these letters around, tied in a bundle with a few others including one from Dorothy, his wife. When he left my flat for America he asked me to look after them because his luggage would be searched and he didn't want the Customs – or his wife – to get hold of them when he was back in California. I warned him that if he left them with me I would read them. He hesitated, then said, 'Rather you than some bastard in the US customs.' So read them I did, and they were a record of an affectionate relationship, with friendship in it as well as warm sexual feeling. They made me like the woman who had written them because their easiness suggested a real intimacy between them rather than the kind of modish self-deception that I had been half expecting. Until the last one – and in that the failure was not Jean's.

It was a letter full of shock and sadness because, out of the blue, he had turned on her in a truly paranoid way, accusing her savagely of spying on black people through him, of using and betraying him. In spite of her pain she wrote with dignity and sense. Reading between the lines I saw that she, like me, had flattered herself that she could soothe and stabilise this difficult man: she was not about to blame him for her own misreading of the situation. Jean Seberg was soon to fall to pieces psychologically, but these letters gave no evidence of anything but a warm and generous nature mixed with enough good sense to save her bacon.

Before they broke Hakim had suffered his mad fit. Things were bad. His wife was angry, refusing to accept his explanation of his affair, and no doubt his group was becoming suspicious too; meanwhile he was becoming more and more hooked, and having to work harder and harder at denying guilt. The 'ugly' son of that beautiful, almost-white mother was getting what his being had always yearned for – delicious 'forgiveness' of his blackness – at a time when it was the last thing he could allow himself to accept.

With all this going on he went, so he told me, to a big Black Power meeting in Detroit. According to his account the meeting exploded into violence, the police broke in, shots were fired, a cop was killed. Hakim used his gun. He was arrested with many others, most of them Panthers, and like the rest of them he had his hands and wrists dusted with a powder that changes colour if a gun has been fired within a certain time before the test. His test was positive. He told me that he got off because he was with the Panthers and they had a sharp lawyer who spotted that the police had been over-eager and had made the tests without some preliminary piece of procedure which by law was necessary. All the tests were declared invalid, all the detained men were released – but the shock had been too much for Hakim and he flipped. As far as he could tell afterwards his behaviour continued to appear normal, but the next thing he knew he was in Paris, and he hadn't the faintest idea how he had got there.

Jean must have organised it, but he never recovered the details or understood how he had been able to travel on a ticket issued in the name of his dog (Ludlow Poindexter) while carrying his own passport. He had kept the ticket cover and showed it to me. He also showed me five or six scruffy pages which he had written in the

Paris hotel where he had 'woken up', in an attempt to clear his mind. They started as a confused effort to sort out reality from dream – had such and such a thing happened, had he sat across a table drinking coffee with so and so, or were these pictures imaginary? Then, with no apparent break, it turned into a passionate and incoherent outcry against the hideousness of life without love: the dreadful fate of being unable to love when loving was the only thing which made life worth living. It was a disconcerting document – to him as well as to me. 'Imagine *me* writing that!' he said. 'I still feel it wasn't me – I wouldn't write that. But it seems that I did.' I was silenced by it, fearing that he would feel insulted if he saw how pitiful I found it.

Jean then carried him off to her house in Spain, and afterwards to Morocco, so that he could rest and recover from what she in her letters called his 'illness' and he remembered bluntly as 'madness'. They had a peaceful and happy time together, though disturbed by distraught telegrams from her husband and his wife, which he had kept and which I saw with the letters (the local telegraph offices must have been agog with excitement). He didn't, however, regain his balance completely. No sooner was he back in the United States than he wrote her the crazy and vituperative letter, her answer to which I read. Facing the music raised by his wife and his friends was presumably too much for him, and the dreadful load of guilt had to be toppled off his shoulders on to hers.

So Hakim had already flipped once; he had his suspect weakness for the occult; and he had moments, anyway, of believing he was God. He also seemed to attribute some kind of magical significance to the Malcolm X hat he always wore, and to his heavy horn-rimmed spectacles which had plain glass in them (Malcolm X wore heavy horn-rimmed spectacles). I thought at first that these were no more than a deliberate attempt to emphasise his likeness to Malcolm; but when a girl once took his hat off his head and put it on her own his sudden rage was alarming, and he said to me afterwards in a very flustered voice: 'The great thing about you and Halé is that *you don't mess with my hat*.' In other words, I knew by the end of his second stay with me that Hakim was a bit mad. But I knew little about mental disturbance (always hard to believe in, anyway, when it attacks someone you like – 'Surely this is some peculiar aberration that will soon go away?'), and he'd been perfectly sane about his book and in all his talk of the past, and never anything but agreeable and friendly towards me. I hoped, therefore, that his mental disturbance came on only from time to time. A wobbly man he certainly was, but given the contentment he was enjoying in Morocco with Halé, might he not be reaching firmer ground? Would he necessarily suffer another crisis? I thought of him by then with great concern, and wished him over his troubles so strongly that I made myself optimistic.

Five

Now for Halé. Her father, Sir Leonard Plugge, was once
a Conservative MP, and rich, but was now neither. The
way she spoke of him was like the way people describe
disasters which have befallen them on holiday: however
dreadful it was at the time they enjoy remembering it as
a horror story. She accused him of nothing worse than
determination to groom her into being the kind of daughter who would do him credit among smart people, which
– she insisted – sickened her; and was never more specific
in her complaints about her childhood than to say that
the household had been 'mad'. Undoubtedly, however,
she thought of herself as having had an extremely unhappy childhood. Perhaps the reason why I never heard
any detail about it was that Hakim was always present
when we were together, and he always held the centre of
the stage. As for the recently circulated rumour that she
was begotten by President Kennedy's father while he
was Ambassador to the UK, I can only suppose that she
had never heard any hint of it. If she had, she might well
not have told me but would surely have told Hakim, and
he would not have been able to resist the temptation to
boast of it. As it was, he several times expatiated on the
grandeur of her father's career – he clearly found it both
bizarre and gratifying that his woman should be the child
of a British Member of Parliament. Had he been able to
claim that she was half-sister of President Kennedy I
would never have heard the end of it.

The only aspect of her upbringing for which she
seemed to be grateful was the French she had learnt
(very well) at the Lycée in Knightsbridge where she

went to school. She married young to a man she knew well, but by the time she met Hakim the marriage was breaking, or had broken, up. She had already bolted once: fallen for a Brazilian, run after him to Rio, and found when she got there that he didn't want her. She stayed in Brazil for a while, living by teaching English and working as an interpreter. Then she made her way to the United States and either her father or her husband sent her a ticket home. Friends of her husband, whom Hakim met before he met her, described her to him as a neurotic and dishonest bitch: she was unhappy, depressed and badly overweight. 'And she *did* use to do wrong,' Hakim told me, without saying how except that she had slept around a good deal. Her husband had tried to make her see a psychoanalyst, and she may have attempted suicide (she did so twice while with Hakim, both times after he had been away and she had gone to bed with another man in his absence). All she said when I asked her what was wrong with her husband from her point of view was 'He's a very weak person'. In spite of her many casual affairs she had never had an orgasm.

To begin with Hakim was delighted with his first patrons in London, but he soon turned against them. He was likely to turn against anyone who befriended him, but his spitefulness about these people, often funny, was not unpersuasive. He did not deny that they had been patient and long-suffering with him, but he felt that they valued their own patience and long-suffering more than they valued him: that they wanted a nigger to be kind to because they were bent on being good. And the wife of one of their friends, after sleeping with him, told someone that he was so desperately in love with her that he trembled in her presence – a fearful insult, in his eyes. He described this woman as a masochist and said that he had disgusted himself by responding to her masochism to the point of hitting her, which she enjoyed. This had rattled him: perhaps he had enjoyed it too, and he

44

was always prudish about any kind of off-beat sex. This woman telephoned him once or twice when he was staying with me, and once he became so angry that he broke the telephone when he hung up, shouting 'They're sick, all of them – they're a sick sick lot!' By the time he met Halé he was ready to like anyone who was disliked by the 'sick sick lot'.

He said that the moment he was in bed with Halé he realised that she was painfully tense, 'So I said to myself take it slowly, this one had better be for her, not me.' The classic marvel happened, she discovered what sex is about, and within three weeks she had lost (so they both insisted and so other people confirmed) about three stone, becoming the elegant, boyish-looking young woman I first met. To both of them this sudden loss of weight had immense significance: he had re-made her, it was a miracle. She became Halé Kimga (an anagram of Hakim and Gale), and took to counting her age from the start of their affair.

It was not only her body that he'd changed. He had also, she insisted, re-created her mentally and spiritually, making her feel secure for the first time in her life, and giving her a sense of purpose. I don't know the nature of the vacuum inside her, or what had caused it, but Hakim certainly filled it. From now on she would work at his side for black people. She had embraced his teaching about what whites have done to blacks (a simplified version of what Malcolm X had taught) with such passion that she wanted to turn herself black – she hated her own white skin and European hair. About her skin she could do nothing beyond expose it to the sun (and she tanned well), but she made him cut off her hair and from then on wore it as short as an old-fashioned boy's (which suited her).

When Hakim began to tell me about all this the word he used most often was 'comical'. 'She's such a comical little girl.' In Morocco – could I beat this! – she refused to use a European-style lavatory, saying she could pee comfortably only on a squatter, like an African. Everything African had become holy to her. After Hakim had given me a funny account of a group of Senegalese diplomats in an airport lounge fanning themselves ostentatiously with their tickets so that everyone could see they were travelling first class, he added, 'Oh man! I could never get away with telling that story in front of Halé!' She was taking Arabic lessons, she was studying the Koran, she had made friends with the women who lived in their street in Agadir so as to learn from them the proper Muslim way to serve her husband. But although Hakim found all this 'comical', he was also proud of it and touched by it. Halé might be funny in her convert's zeal, but he felt that she was on the right track and he had put her there.

He was also proud of her abilities and resourcefulness, her general knowledge and her languages. She was teaching him French (he made pretty good progress, too). They had gone first to Scandinavia, then worked their way down to Agadir driving a beat-up old Ford which kept breaking down, and if it hadn't been for Halé, he said, they wouldn't have made it. She was far better than he was in a crisis. 'When the car gave out in the middle of a desert I started sweating, I can tell you, but not her. She just said "Don't worry, we can rest in the shade of the car and someone will come by sooner or later", and when someone did she knew how to talk to him and he took us to his village and fed us...' She carried her sewing-machine with her and could always run up *dashikis* to sell in the street or to local shops. She made them well – I had one for years – using a yard and a half of cotton for shirt-length garments and three yards for dress-length. (She possessed no other clothes except for a pair of jeans, a leather jerkin and one blue cotton frock with flowers on it.) When they were out of money in Agadir they lived on her *dashikis*, and on paint-jobs she did on shop-fronts and signs, and there were times when she got them money by telling him to keep out of sight and begging. It was she, not he, he told me several times, who was the clever traveller.

'Is she pretty?' I asked. He said he didn't know. 'How can you tell if a person is pretty when you know their face so well?' But she did have a pretty back, he could show me that; and he took from his wallet a photograph of Halé hanging out the washing on their roof in Agadir. She was wearing only a towel wrapped low on her hips, and her back was indeed beautiful, flowing down in a lovely curve to meet hips which were very feminine in spite of her thinness. He kept the snapshot propped up beside him for the rest of the evening, looking at it affectionately from time to time.

'We have so much fun together,' he said. They laughed all the time, and that was something he had never done before. He remembered one of his daughters saying 'Daddy, why don't you ever laugh?' and he guessed that usually he didn't, but he did with Halé. And they never stopped talking. 'The people in Agadir must wonder what in the hell we have to talk about all the time. They see us going down to the beach in the morning, our mouths going a mile a minute, yackety yackety yack, and then about four hours later they see us coming back, our mouths still going a mile a min-ute…' When they got home they left their door on the latch because they felt it wrong to shut out their friends, but all the same they couldn't help their hearts sinking when they heard steps outside, they were so happy talking. Sometimes they talked right through the night. He had never before had a woman with whom he could talk like that. And she was not possessive. She had told him (later she would repeat this to me) that it wouldn't matter if sex died down between them because she loved him in so many other ways: as a teacher, a father, a brother, a friend – 'and even as a god'.

Hakim insisted that he was incapable of loving. Sometimes he said it as a boast, as if such sissiness were beneath him, and sometimes sadly, as though admitting to a shortcoming. Once, after listening to him talking about Halé, I said: 'All right, you don't have to *say* that you love her, but I'm damned if I can see what else you are doing,' and he gave me a sheepish look and stayed silent. I still believe that for at least their first nine months together they were unusually happy.

Six

Before I describe the first time Halé came with Hakim to stay with me I have to write about one more thing: money.

Hakim never asked me for it, but on two occasions I gave him some: once so that he could get back to Morocco, and once so that he could return to the States for good – or so it seemed at the time.

He needed very little money. He and Halé slept where someone offered them a bed, or in their car (the last time they came to England they brought with them an ancient Volkswagen bus of his which was quite liveable-in). They ate once a day, a small meal unless someone gave them a big one. Charles Gooding said he thought he would starve while he was with them. Whenever Hakim made money – the advance on his book or payment for an article – he used it for moving on with, trusting that something would turn up when he reached wherever he was going. In the time I knew him he spent what seemed to me a considerable sum on travelling but very little on living. He lived off the land...and often he was travelling off the land as well, if my reaction to his needs is anything to go by.

After selling his book, for which we gave him an advance of £500 and his American publishers a rather larger sum, he began to dream of earning money by writing. Until then he had contributed an occasional article to the underground press; now he saw himself writing for 'real' newspapers. He would keep himself and Halé in Morocco, and send money to Dorothy, by 'writing articles about Africa'. He was, of course, unable to do anything of the sort, and the little money he had to start with soon ran out.

When he turned up in London, therefore, I couldn't help wondering if I would be stuck with him; and also I worried on his behalf. How on earth would he manage? I watched him bustling about, trying to sell an obviously unsaleable article in order to raise the fare back to Morocco and something to live on for a while when he got there, and I learnt by questioning him that he had failed. So, since he had to get back somehow – I didn't want him with me indefinitely – I offered him the fare plus fifty pounds. He accepted without fuss, pointing out that it would be a miracle if he could ever pay me back; and that, I concluded, must often have been the way he moved on. Someone stumped up, either to get rid of him or because they had become entangled in concern for him. With me, at that time, it was about fifty-fifty.

The second time it was mostly concern, because when I told him that I would pay his fare back to the US he wasn't with me in London so there was no question of being stuck with him. He was still in Morocco. His wife, who was clearly in desperate financial straits, had been telephoning me from Los Angeles to find out where he was, and the thought of this woman stranded with the six children was upsetting. Everything he had told me about Dorothy made her sound an exceptionally likable person – strong, loyal and kind. She was very good-looking, too, and the children were beautiful: he had shown me photographs, speaking of them with pride and of Dorothy with affection and respect, and taking all the blame for the break on himself. So now, when he wrote describing the failure of his Moroccan hopes and saying that like it or not he would have to go home and try to take up his responsibilities again, I was not surprised. I had once heard him speaking to Dorothy and to one of his sons on the telephone, sounding pleased that she had called him (she could have got my number only from him) and paternal to the child – a glimpse of a marriage that had, after all, endured for a long time, through much pain, until his affair with Jean Seberg proved the last straw. A reluctant decision to go home and cope seemed in keeping with the picture he had presented so far.

It was also, of course, in keeping with my feelings on the subject. I had never said to him, 'You ought to go back to your family' because it was none of my business; but he was tuned in to my attitudes well enough to understand that I would think better of him if he did: he knew his virtuous intention would have my support. I had stumped up once before without being asked. He and Halé had now (as became clear later) exhausted the hospitality of Agadir and would starve if they stayed there much longer; the only place he *could* go was home; so I imagine that he trailed his conscience about his family on the chance that I would rise to it and stump up again. Which, as I happened to have more money than usual in the bank at the time, I did. I wrote and told him that he could have £200.

I should add that when he got back to the States he did go home to Dorothy and he did make attempts to raise money for her. He believed his own story enough to act on it as best he could. But in retrospect I'm pretty sure that the story was bred simply by the necessity to move on from Morocco.

Everyone in this story was at some time or another at least a little mad, and my lunacy began now, when on reading his answer to my offer I didn't withdraw it and end the relationship.

I had referred to having a 'nest-egg' out of which I could lend him the money – the word 'lend' being a politeness. His reply began: 'If you have any type of nest-egg enjoy it my darling, enjoy it. You must enjoy it now, with all the things it can do – for *you*. I know you understand that I am not being noble when you have suggested that you might be beautiful enough to *loan* me the fare back to the US to be with Dorothy and the kids …that's nice. But why in the world would you dip into your nest-egg for me? Everything you undertake in this world should give you some degree of satisfaction… Imagine this, if you loaned me some money you'd be out of pocket just by "being nice" for Dorothy and being nice for me. What would you get out of it? I'll tell you – nothing at all.'

Good heavens, I thought, can he be going to refuse it? But there was still a lot of letter to go so I guessed I had better check my relief until I had read more. And indeed I had only to read the next sentence.

'But if – and this is a big if – IF I need the money and you agree to loan it to me – let me come to London and give you a week or weekend that you'll long remember. Plenty of love, plenty of kissing, plenty of fucking – then at least, my darling, you would have some at least of what would make you happy. That, to me, is intelligent. If it comes necessary to dip, and it will [so the 'if' was not so big after all!] enjoy dipping to the utmost. Get the most out of your money. Money is for making you happy, *n'est ce pas*? Then what makes you happy NOW? Why in the world must you wait for that lugubrious "when I'm old"? I hope you understand what I am saying to you, it is just a matter of Jamalian honesty. Sure I need money, sure you are willing to loan me some. That's sweet in any-one's language. But while you loan it, why in the hell can't we also get the fullest from the moment – honestly?'

He then went on to imagine me fearing some risk to my reputation and answered this fear by pointing out that no one need know. 'So you need not risk anything. I will get my loan and that is what I need. I will also be able to make love to you because I want to and so do you. In this way we both achieve exactly what we want.'

Of course, he went on, I could just loan him the money (which I supposed had to be interpreted as just mail him the money) if I'd prefer it. But he was most unlikely to be able to repay the loan, as I must surely know, whereas 'I most certainly can deal with our RIGHT NOW'. And 'if somehow you begin to see yourself as being treated by me like "an old woman who is reduced to buying sex", that, my darling, is your problem. You wrestle with it. I am not a moral person. I like what makes me happy and you make me happy. DECIDE!'

So: I was not to *lend* him money; I was to *give* it to him in exchange for 'a week or weekend' of love-making, thus equalising the burden of gratitude between us!

It took me two readings before I fully grasped this argument, if argument it can be called, partly because of its intrinsic dottiness and partly because the letter – out of which I have picked only some of the clearer passages – was very long and convoluted. And I suppose I ought to regret having to admit that by the time I did grasp it I was beginning to laugh rather than to splutter with indignation. The naiveté of his contortions; the classic guttersnipe assumption that a prick has a market value; the cunning forestalling of the obvious reaction of indignation ('If somehow you begin to see yourself...') – all this nonsense when the silly bastard only needed to say 'Yes thank you'... It struck me as comic. What had gone on in his head? Why did he feel that he had to cook up this long and ridiculous non-argument?

Finally I concluded (rightly, I'm sure) that he hadn't 'cooked it up'. He had really *seen* accepting the money through the mail and accepting it in London after making love as two different things, the second of which would be so valuable to me that it would be worth every penny of £200.

I thought I was going to send him a money order by return of post, but laughter is relaxing. 'Honestly' he had said, 'I want to and so do you'. And if I didn't stand on my dignity, wasn't that true? Would it not in fact be more amusing and agreeable to see him again and to enjoy

53

some more of that delicious love-making, than it would be simply to post a money-order? Yes, of course it would.

I let a couple of days pass to allow for second thoughts, then wrote and told him that I found his letter comic but couldn't deny that it would be more fun if he came to London. Then I cashed a cheque for £200 and put the money, in an envelope, in the bottom left-hand drawer of my dressing-table, stuffing it far to the back. I chose this drawer because it contained nothing but some old wooden beads and two pairs of disused spectacles, dull contents with a film of dust on them from lying undisturbed. I had no reason to suppose that Mrs H, who had been coming twice a week to clean for me for the last three years, was a drawer-opener; but if she ever had felt the temptation to examine my possessions she would long ago have written that drawer off. The reason why I cashed the cheque at once was because I am mean about money and knew that giving this sum away would become more disagreeable the longer I turned it over in my mind. The least painful method was to act at once, while the impulse was still fresh. Once I had taken the money out of my account I could feel that the gift had been made, and could forget it.

There followed several weeks without news from Hakim, during which it occurred to me that in promising me an amorous interlude he'd been promising more than he could perform, because this time he would not be coming to London on his own. The Moroccan adventure was over, he was US-bound for good, so he would be bringing Halé back with him and saying goodbye to her while here. This I knew because we had talked about whether he could take her with him if he had to return, and he had insisted that it was impossible: it would be too hard on her to live his kind of life in the States, and very bad for him to appear with a white mistress when he was already in disgrace with 'his men' over Jean – not to mention that the chief purpose of this return was to pick up his family responsibilities. He had said in a letter, 'I'm trying to brainwash her into accepting that it has to end. Don't know if I'll succeed. I hope so.' If he did pay me a visit, what it would amount to was my having them *both* to stay and then having to keep out of the way while they went through their inevitably painful parting. He would have to focus all his attention on Halé when it came to it...although she *might*, I supposed, stay elsewhere? That seemed unlikely, but when I wondered about it, in one small, almost imperceptible corner of myself there lurked a hope that *if* they came, that's how it would be...

Meanwhile, what were they up to? In the first week or so after writing to him I asked myself that question fairly often, but by the time his silence had lasted a month I'd put it aside. No doubt they would turn up sooner or later – or if they didn't I'd be £200 the richer, which would please me. I don't remember feeling any disappointment as it became increasingly likely that they were not going to show.

The telephone rang about half an hour after I had gone to sleep: a French operator on the line asking for me by name: a person-to-person call. Then an unknown woman's voice: 'Diana? It's Halé here.'

'Why, hullo! Where are you?'

'We're in Paris. I have someone here who would like to speak to you.'

It would be Hakim, I thought; he would have made her put through the call because she spoke French well. But it was another woman's voice, American this time, very soft and caressing.

'Is that Diana? I want so very much to speak with you. My name's Jean Seberg and Hakim Jamal has told me how kind you've been to him. I love Hakim Jamal so I love anyone who is kind to him. I want to say that you must be a very very beautiful person.'

It is not easy – indeed, it is impossible – to reply elegantly to a film star you have never met who wakes you at one-thirty a.m. to tell you in a voice throbbing with theatrical emotion that you are very very beautiful. I thought she must be drunk. Practical questions seemed to be the solution, so I asked if Hakim and Halé were still planning to come to London. 'Perhaps we'll *all* come,' she said. 'I do so long to meet you.' That sounded like an interesting development – into my half-awake head swam images of all of us sunk in chintz-covered armchairs in a suite at the Ritz – or Claridge's? – talking about each other's beauty. When did she think they'd come? 'Quite soon, I expect.' Was Hakim there? 'No, he's out just now.' Then there was some more and even more extravagant waffle about my nature (ought I to say 'How kind of you' – 'No no, you exaggerate' – 'Not nearly so beautiful as you'???), and at last she was ready to say goodnight and hang up.

By that time I was fully awake and my wits had collected. But this, I thought, is marvellous! He has made his peace with the woman, he's in clover. On which followed the words 'And I can keep my money!' and the passing thought that if Jean could have overheard them she'd have taken back at least one 'very'.

How, I wondered, did Halé fit in? The two women must be in cahoots, telephoning me in his absence like that – telephoning me behind his back? The more I pondered the conversation, the more likely it seemed that I had been given my marching orders. Jean was staking her claim on him and Halé was supporting her: that would mean that Jean's generosity was at work again. Yes, Hakim's problems were solved, and very likely those of his wife as well. *Clever* old pussy-cat, I thought as I went back to sleep.

*

A week later, however, there was a call from Hakim who sounded furtive, as though he were hoping not to be overheard. He said that he was angry with the two women for calling me, and that what was going on was 'indescribable'. I was to expect him 'before too long'. And ten days later he arrived.

I was at the office at the time, so the people who live downstairs from me let him in. 'I slept last night in the car,' he told me on the telephone, 'because I got in late and didn't want to disturb you. I only just made it – my car's on its last legs. Shall I bring yours down to the office and fetch you after work?' *I*, not *we*. I didn't ask myself why I refrained from saying 'Where's Halé?', and understood only later that it was because I didn't want to show him that I cared – which must mean that I did. His *I* instead of *we* had given me a jump of pleasure distinctly more marked than I expected, and I had reacted by disguising the fact. It was mortifying – only slightly so, but still mortifying – to have caught myself out in this degree of involvement when I had thought myself actually pleased that his 'bargain offer' had evaporated.

As I said earlier, I had realised from the start that Hakim had an extraordinary nose for hypocrisy or reserve so that the only simple way of dealing with him was by being open. Now I had not been quite open. I had got off on the wrong foot with him, which would affect the next few days to a surprising extent.

The process began at once. There wasn't any food in my flat, so I must go out and buy something for supper. How many would I buy for? I couldn't be certain that Halé wouldn't be there, so the sensible decision would have been to buy for three just in case; instead of which I kept telling myself 'Well, he *did* say "I" ', and I bought steak and vegetables for two – and why would I bet on Halé's absence unless I wished for it?

Everyone else had left the office by the time the bell rang, so I answered the door myself. There was Hakim waiting with arms outstretched to sweep me into a dramatic embrace; and there at his shoulder was a tall girl wearing a long white sheepskin coat, looking like Greta Garbo disguised as a Russian princeling, 'Why, Halé!' I exclaimed, passing from his embrace to hers with what I was sure was impeccable smoothness, while inside myself I heard, only too clearly: 'Oh fuck, she's here after all'; and the next second I was thinking I mustn't let him see that I bought only two steaks.

He was watching me bright-eyed, and I knew at once that he was looking for my disappointment: he had picked up that unasked 'Where's Halé?' over the phone and he was enjoying the situation, blast him. He had set up a little trap for me and by trying to dodge it I'd fallen in. And went on falling. Because instead of saying 'But love, why didn't you tell me you were both here? I've only bought supper for two so now we'll have to stop on the way home and get some more', I said, 'We'll have to stop on the way home and buy something for supper.' I'd nip into the shop and get one more steak while they thought I was getting three. He'd got me rattled.

And then it turned out that they had already bought food and had left it cooking in my kitchen. At which point, when I caught myself thinking, Now I'll have to unpack my shopping in such a way that they don't see those two steaks, I drew the line. This was becoming too ridiculous. 'Oh come on,' I told myself then, 'what the hell does it matter if he *does* see? The old bastard will flatter himself that I was wanting to have him to myself, and so I was, so what! Forget it!' And when we reached the flat I gave my shopping bag to Halé, who had said that she would finish the cooking while Hakim and I talked, and let her get on with unpacking it.

Seven

Hakim poured me a whisky and himself a Coke, and we left the door between the sitting-room and the kitchen open so that Halé could join in our talk. She was instantly at home, seeming to know by instinct where everything was and working with a charming deftness: Hakim had been right when he praised her competence. And she behaved towards me as though she had adopted as a matter of course his affection for me and his knowledge of my ways. He was the narrator of their adventures in Paris, she the chorus, chipping in with comments and reminders.

It became necessary for them to go to Paris, he said, when he heard that Jean, who had recently lost a baby almost immediately after its birth, was having a breakdown. 'I realised she needed me, and in spite of everything that had happened I couldn't let her down.' I guessed this to mean that he saw a chance to renew their friendship at a time when he was frantic for money, which seemed thoroughly undignified but not – from his point of view – unreasonable. To make the journey they sold typewriter, tape machine, sewing machine, most of their clothes – almost everything but the car. It took them over a week to get from Morocco to Paris because of breakdowns, and when they arrived they found no one at Jean's house.

She was divorced from Romain Gary, her novelist husband, but was still on fairly friendly terms with him, so they went to his house for news of her. She was in Spain, he said; so they retired to a café to discuss their next move, and there by chance met a maid of Jean's who knew Hakim from the days of his affair with her employer, and she told them that Jean was not in Spain but in a Paris nursing-home, very ill. She gave them the address and they went there at once.

Hakim went in and found Jean 'as nutty as a fruit-cake'. He told her that her husband and the doctors were up to no good – look how Gary had lied about where she was! – but now he, Hakim, had come to cure her and all would be well. She ordered her bags to be packed and went home to her house with Hakim and Halé. One of the bags, a small red one, she insisted on carrying herself because she suspected that the Black Panthers had placed a bomb in it and she refused to expose anyone else to the risk of being blown up.

Her recent history, as Hakim told it, was that late in her pregnancy she had become deeply depressed and had taken an overdose of sleeping pills. She had been rushed to a clinic, where the baby was born and soon afterwards died. During this ordeal she had been surrounded by a bodyguard wished on her by the Black Panthers (Hakim made no attempt to explain the clinic's allowing this), who had taken her under their wing in the belief that the baby would be black, and had frightened her out of her wits by stationing one of their men in her room all the time. He sat in her room night and day until her nerve broke and she begged to have her bed moved out into a hallway so that there would be other people around. She was terrified that the fact that the child was not black would bring down the Panther's wrath.

It did not occur to Hakim or Halé to suspect that these threatening figures existed only in Jean's mind, but Hakim had his own ideas about their identity. When at one point I said incredulously 'The *Panthers*?' he replied: 'Of course not. Hangers-on. Rabble. Man, how those boys have been taking her!'

After the baby died Jean became obsessed with it. She had photographs taken of it in its coffin and tapes made of the funeral, and these she brooded over, and made other people brood over, for hours on end. Presumably it was this morbid obsession combined with delusions such as her belief in the bomb planted in her suitcase that had landed her in the nursing-home.

Mysteriously, by the time Hakim reached Paris the 'Panthers' had been routed, and now her entourage consisted of 'the Masons'. The Masons were hanging about the nursing-home, her house was always full of them and she was completely under their influence. As soon as the Masons appeared in the story a warning light began to flicker in my mind, and Hakim's triumph over them made it flicker even more. These enigmatic figures had, of course, constantly given signs and uttered passwords; but they were low-grade Masons, a shoddy lot, and he had confounded them by always coming back with a sign or password which showed them he was more deeply initiated than they were. They might command Powers, but he commanded greater Powers, so they split. 'It didn't take me long to get rid of *them*, did it?' he said to Halé, and they both laughed with pleasure at the scene they were remembering. Meanwhile I was beginning to feel that I was looking at two images blurred together on one photographic plate. There had, no doubt, been hangers-on of some sort there, and they had been ousted by Hakim; but who or what they were and exactly why they left was impossible to discern.

It seemed, however, possible that 'the Masons' had been taking Jean just as brazenly as 'the Panthers', because the poor woman had obviously become easy game for takers. When she saw that Hakim had delivered her from her tormenters she declared that he, her only love, must stay with her for ever, and she appointed Halé her secretary.

So she had welcomed Halé? I said. Very kindly to start with, Hakim replied, because she could see that he wanted her to; but she had not been able to keep it up and before long she was openly hostile, referring to Halé as 'that slave you keep upstairs'. I asked Halé, 'But wasn't that horrible?' and she answered with feeling 'Perfectly unspeakable'. And it wasn't only Jean. The servants soon spotted what Jean felt, and after that, whenever anything went wrong – if something was lost or broken – it was always Halé's fault. She did not, however, seem to have questioned the necessity of prolonging their stay in Jean's house.

Hakim had seen at once that Jean's trouble was that her fantasy world had taken over and was obscuring the real world. To cure her he must destroy her fantasies, and he started the very first night. Had she not told him in the past, he asked her, that she had sometimes played with the idea of sleeping three in a bed? She admitted it. All right, he said they would now make that fantasy real. They would go upstairs to bed with Halé and he would fuck both of them. Into bed they got, and all of them loathed it. 'So *there* you are,' he said to Jean. 'You thought you wanted to do that but now you know that you didn't and we've got rid of it'; and he took her down to her own room and rewarded her with some good private love-making. The next day he reminded her – or told her – that she used to say that she liked being sucked. 'I don't go in for that kind of thing,' he told me, 'so I got a boy to come in, promised him a good dinner and a little cash and he was looking forward to it.' But when the boy arrived Jean began to cry and said that Hakim was treating her like a whore. 'So *there* you are,' he said again. 'It was only a fantasy, wasn't it? You don't really want it at all.' And he sent the surprised and disappointed boy away.

But the chief fantasy he had to destroy was the one about loving her dead baby. After he had seen her putting on her ceremony of mourning over the tapes and photographs, making her household sit round and weep with her, he knew he had to stop that. So he took the tape and pictures away from her and told her he was going to destroy them. She wept, screamed, tried to scratch his face, but he persisted. It was ridiculous play-acting, he told her; she hadn't loved the child at all. 'Yes, I told her, you look at those pictures again – look at it! A hideous little lump of flesh, a foetus, a *thing*. You never loved that *thing* – nobody could love it.' She cried all day, but he went on and on at her until at last she tore up the photographs, gave him the tape and admitted that she had not really loved the baby. Again he made love to her as a reward.

These 'successes' whetted his appetite for the role of healer, and he began to take her through her childhood, forcing her to admit guilts and fears, then 'releasing' her from them. The more he described, the more evident it became that he had been wishing these guilts and fears on to the wretched woman and brainwashing her into admitting to them whether she had experienced them or not so that he could have something to 'cure'. He had bludgeoned her for hours with the scraps of half-knowledge about psychotherapy that he had picked up from magazine articles and so on, and she, far too sick to defend herself, had let him do it. The story (both as he told it and as I envisaged it) was so bizarre that I was fascinated and wanted more and more, but at the same time it was frightening. He had obviously become a good deal more aggressively mad than he had been when I last saw him.

There were moments when the two images on the plate came together. 'That house was unspeakable,' he said, 'a real madhouse,' and Halé concurred. It had been an exhausting turmoil of people coming and going, plans made and unmade, never a moment's peace. She was always whirling them all from place to place – they only had to decide on a quiet night at home in order to find themselves in some nightclub – and when they both groaned at the memory of how irritating and tiring it had been, I was able for a moment to share their vision.

From one of those nightclub jaunts Hakim had brought a scar – or rather two scars, literal ones. Jean had been sitting opposite him at a narrow table when suddenly he noticed her puffing violently at her cigarette. 'I knew at once what she was up to. I thought Jesus! – but if that's what she's going to do I must let her...' and he left his hand where it was, flat on the table, palm down. She ground her cigarette into the back of it and he didn't move. She puffed again and burnt another hole, this one in the flesh between his thumb and forefinger. By then, he said, he was almost fainting, but still he didn't move his hand (and this must have been true because both wounds were neat, deep and unblurred). 'I understood, you see, that this wasn't Jean. It was something evil inside her and I had to let it come out – I had to bring it out.' Then she began to cry and he went off to an outpatients' department of some hospital to have his hand dressed, and when he got back 'she was sobbing all over everybody, telling them what she'd done to the person she loved best in the world'. Halé shook her head over this incident, compressing her lips. I got the impression that left to herself she would gladly have snatched the cigarette from Jean's hand and ground it into her eyes, but that she still hadn't questioned Hakim's superior wisdom.

While all this was going on Romain Gary and Jean's doctors must have been at their wits' ends. Gary came round to the house on several occasions, only to be confounded by Hakim's 'debating' (a scene I could clearly envisage). Finally he must have decided that his best hope lay in attacking the invader on his own level. He called Hakim urgently to his house and told him that he had received information that the police were about to move in on him. It might be too late – but he had managed to get hold of a *laisser-passer* which would make officials speed Hakim on his way out of the country if he used it quickly, within the next two days. Hakim showed me this document, and splendidly official-looking it was, but although he'd decided to take no chances and had left at once, he was uneasy. 'I don't know what all that was about,' he said. 'There was some funny business going on there, I'm pretty sure.' Jean had been rushed back into the nursing-home the day he left.

At the end of this story, which had taken us through supper and well into the night, Halé started to yawn and said that she must go to bed. She asked if she could have a bath, and when I came back into the sitting-room after getting her a towel I said to Hakim that I must make their bed up for them. 'Make Halé's bed,' he said. 'I'm sleeping with you.'

'Oh no you're not, love,' I said. 'I've never felt less like sleeping with anyone,' and was glad to observe that the words had come out spontaneously. Apart from the fact that I was shocked that he should suggest our sleeping together under Halé's nose, this lunatic confounder of 'Masons' and healer of sick film stars had superimposed himself on the Hakim who had existed in my head until then and had driven out even the smallest and most secret wish to make love with him.

He didn't argue, and while I was making the bed in the spare-room I thought he was probably relieved. No doubt he had felt obliged to keep his promise to me, but I had gathered – although he had not yet been explicit about it – that he was intending, as I had expected, to go back to the States alone. So these days in London would indeed be taken up by his parting from Halé, and he would surely rather be with her than with me or anyone else.

When I had finished the bed it occurred to me that he might not have told Halé that he was to get money from me: most likely he had, but if he had not he wouldn't want her to see him taking it, so I had better hand it over while she was in the bathroom. 'Oh by the way,' I said, 'I've got that money for you,' and I went into my bedroom to fetch it. It wasn't there.

Perhaps I had pushed it so far back in the drawer that it had fallen through into the body of the dressing-table. I pulled the drawer right out and peered into the cavity, but there was nothing there. Then, controlling rising agitation by breathing slowly, I took everything out of the drawer and removed the lining-paper: nothing; and nothing in the other three drawers, or in my glove drawer, or in my stocking drawer. I knew perfectly well where I had put the money but was telling myself that I might be mistaken – it was the meaningless scrabble of panic. Mrs H, the cleaning woman? But there was no conviction in the question. I had not really chosen that 'safe' drawer as a precaution against Mrs H, only as a gesture towards being sensible because people are supposed to be sensible with money. There was no question of believing that Mrs H had stolen £200. But the £200 had gone.

Hakim said 'What's wrong?' as soon as I came through the door – I felt I had gone pale, and I probably had. I told him, and he said the kind of thing people always say in such circumstances: are you sure you put it there, when did you put it there, think back and reconstruct exactly what you did. 'Look,' I said, going back to my room with him at my heels, 'it was in there, right at the back – I *know* it was there'; and I added that I could not believe that Mrs H had taken it.

'Well, it isn't there now, is it?' he said. 'Perhaps you've forgotten what you did with it,' and I heard in his voice that he was not believing me. He didn't believe the money had ever been there. He was thinking that this was my way out of giving it to him when it came to the point.

Halé came in from the bathroom, and she too said at once 'What's wrong?' – 'Some money has disappeared,' he said, but in an offhand way, and again I went through it, pulling out drawers, racking my brains for an explanation, with every second becoming more sharply aware that he was humouring me. Halé had the look of someone who knows that she ought to be concerned but can't help feeling slightly bored by all the fuss because there is nothing she can do to help, while he was using a 'play along with her just to be kind' manner which was rapidly adding rage to my distress.

It also came near to shaking me. I am in fact absent-minded. I have often 'lost' things which weren't lost, failed to see things which were not hidden. Once, for quite a long time, I did employ a cleaner who took things – rings and scarves and so on – and could never bring myself to feel sure that she had taken them because I knew so well how capable I was of losing them. Could I, I asked myself now, conceivably have done no more than *think* of taking the money out of the bank and putting it in that drawer, and be remembering the thought as an act? But although the unspoken scepticism with which Hakim was filling the room pushed me to the point of asking that question, I knew that the answer was no. I had cashed that cheque (as, indeed, my bank statement was to prove) and had put it in that drawer and nowhere else. It had been stolen either by Mrs H or by Hakim and Halé.

I shall jump ahead now and say what I later decided must have happened. I decided that Halé took the money. They had been in the flat for some hours before coming to pick me up, and it was no secret that they had been into my bedroom because they had to take my spare car-key out of the box on my dressing-table where I keep it. I had seen as soon as Halé went into the kitchen that she knew where everything was. She had certainly poked about – in addition to which she had a 'nose'. And the better I came to know her the more certain I was that Halé would do *anything* if she believed it would help Hakim or if it would keep her with him. Before I saw the last of them I suspected that if Hakim had told her to kill someone she would have done it.

He was the less likely suspect simply because he knew that I was going to give him that money. Seeing it in the drawer, he'd have grinned and envisaged with satisfaction the acting out of the 'script' he had planned for us, or so I feel: I don't see him choosing to mess that script up. But Halé had the shadow of their parting hanging over her. No doubt she could hope to persuade him that she could cope with the problems involved in living with him in the United States, but if there were simply no money for her fare... . Solve that one, and she would be at least halfway there.

If Halé took the money Hakim must, of course, have known about it sooner or later, and must have accepted her act. But I doubt that he was the one who put his hand in the drawer, or even that he told her to do it. Probably he twigged what had happened as soon as I told him it had vanished, and persisted in hinting that I had never put it there because he couldn't think of any other way to cover up for her.

Or was he 'operating'? If so he was doing it with extraordinary skill, sizing up my reaction with uncanny exactness. Because in the tumult of distressing emotions churning in my head, by far the strongest one was anger that he should suspect me of setting up an elaborate lie to camouflage meanness. My vanity found this instantly unacceptable (perhaps it cut near the bone? I *had* been having twinges of meanness about that money), and my response was determination to prove him wrong. The simple blow of the money's disappearance and the misery of having to suspect either them or Mrs H were bad enough, but this unspoken insult, unanswerable because it was unspoken, was worse. I'll show the bastard,

I was thinking. Just as soon as the bank is open on Monday - this was Friday evening – I'll cash another fucking £200 pounds and rub his sneering nose in it: a reaction which seems to me in retrospect so idiotic that I find it hard to believe that he can have foreseen it – can have stolen the first lot of money with the calculated intention of manoeuvring me into producing more. Surely he cannot have had such an acute sense of my nature as to know for sure that I would be such a fool?

Eight

Many people, having concluded that they had been robbed by Y, would proceed to take action against Y. I do not know why the state of mind leading to such action is not at my command, but it is not. What I would do next – not what I would *want* to do or would *decide* to do, but inevitably what I would do – is behave as though it were possible for money to dematerialise. I knew this, so when – instead of working out the above scenario and pondering what to do about it – I said: 'Oh come on, sitting around talking about this isn't going to help – we'd better go to bed', I was wanting to hurry myself on through a night of sleep to a more comfortable mood in which I could feel: money gone from drawer – too bad – let's forget it.

But I woke depressed next day, all the same. It wasn't going to be any fun having them in the flat. First there was the disconcerting dislocation between Hakim's attitude to his own behaviour in Paris and the very disagreeable picture of it I had gained from his account; then there was the wretched business of the money; and now, no doubt, they would have to start thrashing out the question of Halé's future and for the next two or three days would be filling the place with gloom and agitation. I was glad that they were not up by the time I went out to do my Saturday morning shopping, and I made it last as long as I could.

And sure enough, when I got home they were sitting across my hearth-rug from each other, looking very unhappy. I said that I was sorry they didn't drink, because it was obvious that they needed cheering up, and

Hakim asked should Halé go out and get us some hash? They had been smoking kif in Agadir and resented having to pay London prices for it, but a joint or two would do us good today. I agreed, and Halé went off on her mission while I cooked lunch. She looked lovely in her sweeping white coat (it was Jean's coat, which she had given to Hakim because he hadn't got one, but he'd passed it on to Halé because he detested wearing fanciful clothes). It was not only her proportions, her long neck and the set of her head, and the tan she'd brought back from Morocco. It was also the sweetness of her friendly smile and the way it lit up her long-shaped, thick-lashed, speckled grey-green eyes. She was an uncommonly attractive-looking girl, and since at that stage I was putting the vanished money firmly out of my mind, I had no trouble feeling sympathy with her in her painful situation of facing separation from a man for whom she obviously lived.

Hakim, on the other hand, was beginning to feel like trouble. He was looking morose and was in one of his dottier moods. 'I want you to know,' he kept saying, 'that I understand.'

'Understand what?'

'Just understand. I *understand*. Do you see what I mean? I *understand*.' And he fixed me with a gaze of fierce intensity and significance – though what it signified he wouldn't say.

'OK love – you understand,' I said flippantly, returning to the kitchen, but I wasn't feeling flippant. He was on his God kick, that was for sure; it was God's omniscience he was trying to convey to me.

After lunch we lit up. In the next eight hours I smoked only a little – perhaps two joints – but they smoked a great deal.

They had gone back to their seats opposite each other, while I sat like a spectator, somewhat back from them and halfway between them. When it became evident, as it did at once, that they were going to plunge into the question of their parting, I thought of going out of the room to allow them privacy. My first reaction to this thought was but why the hell should *I* go out of my own sitting-room? If they want to be private they can take themselves off somewhere else; and later I became so absorbed in the spectacle they provided that nothing would have shifted me. Besides which, a curious feeling that *I was supposed to be there* as audience soon took over. I came to feel that if I left the room I would disturb what was happening as much as I would if I interrupted by speaking. The hash must have played a part in this, but it wasn't only the hash. I *was* supposed to be there – Hakim wanted me there.

The conversation, it was clear, had begun while I was out shopping. She knew for sure by now that he wanted her to stay in England when he went back to the States; he knew that being parted from him seemed like death to her. He was undertaking an elaborate attempt to make her change her mind.

He leant back in his chair, very still – it was character-istic of him to remain physically relaxed while talking, even if he became angry enough to shout; she slid off her chair and sat cross-legged on the floor, looking up at him, her eyes never leaving his face. Slowly and care-fully he expounded all the arguments against her going with him. They would have no money. They would often go hungry and dirty and cold. They would usually have to sleep in the car. When he was with black friends she would either have to keep away or she would have to face his friends hating her and despising him for being with her. She couldn't be with him at all when he was at home with Dorothy – and that, as she well knew, was where he would have to be for most of the time. Whereas in England, where she still had friends, and her mother, she could earn money easily and make a new life for herself. She was too intelligent to want to be someone's shadow all her life. The teaching would be spread more widely if she worked separately from him.

When she had a counter-argument she produced it. She had never minded discomfort or sleeping in the car, and it was nonsense for him to talk about her mother when he knew how she loathed her family and that he had become all the family she wanted. When she had no answer she came back stubbornly with, 'All I know is that I want to be with you.'

Then he would say, 'All right – it's you who want to come, so let's leave the ball in your court. *You* tell *me* how we'd manage.' Each time this happened her face would light up and she'd outline some plan; and each time he would answer it with a long, detailed, ruthlessly realistic projection of what was really likely to happen if they did that. He seemed to become a cold embodiment of abrasive common sense – there was nothing fanciful or rhetorical in his talk – and she would fail and droop, and come back again to 'All I know is that I want to be with you.'

'Listen,' he said after about two hours: 'Tell me your name; come on, tell me your name.'

'Halé Kimga!' she said defiantly.

'No, tell me your real name.' This she resisted for at least ten minutes, and her breaking was the first time she wept. She flung herself across to him, buried her face in his lap and whispered 'Gale-Ann Benson', then began to sob desperately, while he sat quite still except for the hand which was gently stroking her hair, staring down at her but looking as though he weren't seeing anything.

After that she was crying more often than not, mostly silently, the tears streaming unnoticed down her face as she gazed at him. Round and round they went, over and over the same ground, with slight variations. Whenever he played the 'ball in your court' trick she would stop crying and her face would light up again; whenever he shot one of her proposals down her tears would flow.

Several times he got her to the point of granting that it would be sensible for her to stay in England, and once she said 'If you order me not to come with you, I'll stay.' It seemed, however, that he had set his heart on getting her to *want* to stay. To me it was obvious from the start that he would never achieve this: he could probably make this girl do anything he liked except for this one thing: feel that she wanted to give him up.

He's chicken, I thought: he doesn't want the responsibility of taking her so he's determined to do everything he feels he ought to do to make her stay behind; but on the other hand he doesn't want to go without her so he's setting himself a target he can't possibly reach. Or had he, on the contrary, set himself so difficult a target because he wanted to prove that he had enough power over her to reach it? Sometimes, as he ground on and on at her, I thought that must be it; but when at one desperate moment she cried out 'If I knew for sure that you didn't want me…' and he said gently 'How can I say that? You know that I depend as much on you as you do on me,' my first supposition seemed the more probable one.

Various interesting things came out. Their beloved Agadir, for instance, and their friends there: the previous evening they had referred to it as the unsullied idyll he had described on his earlier visits; but now, when one of Halé's proposals was that he should change his mind and return to Morocco instead of going to America, he asked her harshly, 'And how do you suggest we face Ali and Mustafa Amin after what we did to them?' and it transpired that even when they'd sold all their possessions they had not been able to pay their rent or their debts and had had to do a moonlight flit on people who trusted them. It came out, too, that an 'illness' of Halé's in Agadir, of which I had heard, had really been a suicide attempt. While he had been staying with me the second time, she had run out of money and had slept with 'the Caid' to get some. 'No,' he said, 'I'm not blaming you for what you did, although it was silly. You should have known that I'd understand you wouldn't have slept with him unless you'd thought it would help me. You should have known that, so what you did was unnecessary and stupid, and it lost you five days of Paradise, didn't it?' She didn't question this version of what had happened, but I, watching her complete subservience to him, wondered what he had in fact done and said when he learnt about 'the Caid'. I remembered his telling me that once before, while they were still living in London, she had made an attempt at suicide because she was ashamed of sleeping with some other man in his absence, and it seemed likely that on these occasions he had seen fit to punish her before forgiving and 'understanding'.

Another of Halé's proposals – one for raising enough money to make her independent of him for a time in the States – was 'Well, then, why don't we try J?' J was a very rich woman who had been one of Hakim's first patrons in London. I supposed that by 'try' Halé meant ask her for a loan or gift, but no; Hakim's answer was 'Ach – now you're talking like a real fool. That woman's husband doesn't give a fuck who she fucks, and she knows it. All they'd do is reach for the phone and call the police – if you can't do better than that you'd better give up.' What Halé was suggesting was blackmailing J by threatening to tell her husband that she had slept with Hakim. She accepted his argument, but her grief became sullen for a while: she would have liked to blackmail J.

This exhausting spectacle lasted for eight hours, during which my identification with Halé became more and more intense: identification not with her passion for Hakim but with the pain she was suffering in front of my eyes at the prospect of losing him. She was a crazy girl in love with a crazy man, but their craziness would

75

make no difference to her feelings if she was left without him. It was years since I had lost the most important of my lovers, and a very long time since I had remembered the sensations of that loss; but now, watching Halé's weeping face, those sensations returned. I knew – I could feel – what she was feeling: without Hakim her life would not be worth living and that was not a turn of phrase but the literal truth. He was trying to make her endure a pain which she could not stand, and I couldn't stand it either: I was crying too, I suddenly realised. My face was quite wet.

It was the hash, I suppose. Like most people I knew at that time, I had smoked cannabis, though not often because usually it did less for me than a whisky and water would have done. Twice, however, it had seemed worthwhile; on both occasions because it had intensified my response to something. The first time I was listening to Bach's *St Matthew Passion* and had enjoyed the magical experience of hearing the music originate in my own head; the second time I had made love and again the whole experience had seemed to originate within me, this time in my cunt. Never again had the drug affected me in that way, and it did not occur to me as I watched Halé that it was doing so now, but in retrospect I can see no other explanation for my feelings.

They became too much for me: I'd had enough of this horrible room, so heavy with grief. I must escape from it and go to bed.

I had not been in my bedroom five minutes before there was a tap on the door and there was Halé, sent to fetch me back. 'You must come back – you must. We need you.' She didn't say that she was acting on Hakim's instructions, but it was obvious. I refused. It was past midnight, I was tired, I didn't want any more of it. She persisted. 'Look, I'll wait while you get into something more comfortable – put this on...' and she wrapped me gently and affectionately in my dressing-gown, cajoling, kissing my cheek. 'Just for fifteen minutes, then we'll all go to bed. Just for one last cup of tea.' I gave way.

She must make the tea, I said, thinking that at least their dialogue had been broken up; and when I returned to the sitting-room and took what had been Halé's seat opposite Hakim, he gave me a sardonic look and said: 'Now tell me: why did you think that I wasn't going to take Halé with me to the States?'

'*You're going to take her!*' I cried, jumping out of my chair in delight. It astounded me at the time and it astounds me now, even taking the hash into account: the intensity with which I had shared her pain, and with which now, at a word, her relief and joy shot through me.

'Sit down,' he said. 'Of course I'm taking her. I always was going to take her. Halé knew that. It wasn't *Halé* who doubted.'

'Then what on earth has been going on all day? What were you…why did you…' I was catching up on it: the absurdity of that gruelling day if he'd really been meaning to take her all the time; or the outrageousness of what he was saying now, if he had not been meaning to. And apart from Halé's feelings, how dared he drag *me* through all that as a spectator if it was for nothing? What did he *mean*, he was always going to take her!

He then said 'Diana, stop pretending. You don't have to pretend any more because I *understand*. I told you earlier that I *understand*, didn't I?'

'Understand what, for Christ's sake?'

'I understand why you did what you did last night.'

And what I had done last night, he explained while I sat dumb-founded, was leave my body and take possession of Halé's. I could deny it if I liked but my denial would make no difference to the fact. He could tell me the exact time when I'd done it. It was when I had come to him in the bathroom, crying.

'But I didn't come to you in the bathroom.'

Yes, I had done so – in Halé's body. It was the crying

which had given the game away, because why would Halé cry? She had no reason to cry. I had, of course – good reason. I had been wanting him. I mustn't make myself look silly by denying it now. 'I ordered Halé to look in your shopping bag,' he said, 'and she reported that you'd bought only two steaks – you were wanting an evening alone with me.' Then, because Halé was there, out of foolish 'English good manners' I had turned him away from my bed although I was dying to fuck with him; and I was going to lose him when he left for the USA. I had gone into Halé's body so that I could sleep with him that night.

It was creepy to have it confirmed that I'd been right about the previous evening: that he *had*, as I had felt, picked up my attempt to pretend that I didn't want him when really, before his madness put me off, I did want him more than I had expected; that he, too, had been 'playing the steak game'. If it hadn't been for that I would have felt in less of a turmoil, more impatient and less alarmed by his lunacy. I did indeed have a strong feeling of 'Oh no! This is *too much!*'; but there was also an under-current of real dismay that he had so unerringly fastened on what had been an underlying truth. And what he was now making out of it – that, I saw, might become frightening. He was glaring, his face had gone ugly and his voice was hectoring – he had started to *look* mad in a way I hadn't seen before, and I felt that I ought to start being careful. He might be about to slip right away from reason, into some unpredictable state in which voices might tell him to do mad things, or he might feel bound to act against some threat. I had never felt in the least scared of Hakim before, and I was never to feel it again, but then I suddenly felt 'Watch it! you can't tell how he may go...' But how did one set about 'being careful' in such circumstances? Better let him run on, and take the first chance to break the session up and shunt us all into bed.

So instead of telling him he was talking nonsense, I said that I found it impossible to comment on what he was telling me because it made no sense to me: all I knew about last night was that I'd gone to sleep soon after getting into bed and had slept soundly all night. That allowed him to argue that my soul had been up to all kinds of things that my conscious mind had chosen to ignore, and I felt angry at playing along with his delusion even that much; but I was too exhausted and too alarmed to join battle with him.

He could give me proof, he said: I hadn't known the 'secret words'. He and Halé had words which meant special things to them, last night he had used them, and the woman in bed with him had taken no notice of them. And furthermore this crying woman who didn't know the words had been unable to come when they made love: how could I deny all that proof?

Poor Halé, I thought, so unhappy, not even able to play their games or respond to his body any more. (I had a flash of remembering a farewell love-making I'd once been through, and how dead my body had become because what was the use of it when so soon we were going to be parted?) And at the same time I felt a twitch of indignation that he'd taken frigidity as proof that it was me! Didn't he remember that my response had been lively enough before? But down with that ridiculous twitch of vanity! An attentive silence was the thing.

'Look,' he said, 'I'll demonstrate. *Sayonaro!*' Halé was still in the kitchen, but the door was open. Instantly she put down whatever she was holding, came running in, threw her arms round his neck and covered his face with kisses. 'There, you see, she's herself now, and she knows it,' he said. 'That's our word for "kiss me" and last night she didn't even hear it.'

I watched Halé as she poured the tea. Her eyes were still swollen and red, but her expression had become so calm and happy that it was hard to take their condition as evidence of weeping. I certainly felt far more battered than she looked. He kept interjecting '*Sayonaro!*' into his talk, and each time she jumped up to kiss him with delighted laughter. She was to write in her diary: 'On Friday night Diana took possession of my body' – no more about it than that, just one fact among others, such as that the car's brakes would have to be repaired and that she'd made an appointment with Hakim's agent.

I had begun to feel not just tired but actually ill – a diffuse physical malaise as though I were starting flu. Finally this overcame caution and I decided to go off to bed whether he liked it or not – and anyway, the '*Sayonara*' demonstrations appeared to have calmed him down a bit. 'Well,' I said, 'you go on thinking what you like – I can't stop you and if you want to believe that I took possession of Halé it does me no harm. And now – goodnight. I really am going to bed this time.' And this time he let me go.

The next day, Sunday, I woke late after sleeping heavily, but I still felt so tired that I wondered if I really was beginning flu. I decided to take the papers back to bed with me and stay there for the rest of the morning in the hope that if I didn't appear they would go out. The thought of seeing them again seemed unbearable, but because he had formerly been such a considerate guest I assumed that if my behaviour made it clear that I wanted to be left alone he would leave me alone.

I was incredulous, therefore, when soon after I had heard them stirring he knocked on my door and came straight in without waiting for an answer, followed by Halé carrying a tray of tea. I told them I didn't want it and was going to stay where I was. No, he said, I mustn't be so unsociable, they were looking forward to more talk. 'Well, I'm *not*,' I said, to which he replied that after I'd had a cup of tea I'd feel better. 'Oh do leave me alone,' I said. 'I'm feeling ill – I think I'm getting flu.' I could hear myself sounding sulky and pettish, and couldn't understand why my manner was falling in with his idea of how I was reacting, instead of with my own. He said humouringly that there was no hurry, they would wait for me, then sat down on my bed and began to read the *Observer*. Halé took a colour supplement and settled down on the floor, cross-legged as usual.

This was one of the occasions in my life – not many – when I've felt hamstrung by being 'well brought up'. It doesn't incapacitate one in serious engagements, but in small skirmishes it can leave one absurdly helpless: if someone is rude or inconsiderate in a way which *would never have occurred to me*, I am unable to find an appropriate reaction. I simply couldn't believe that they weren't going to leave me alone in my bedroom when I'd asked them to, but what I couldn't believe was evidently happening, and a lifetime's conditioning to practise and expect a modicum of good manners inhibited my fury. 'GET OUT OF MY ROOM!' I was yelling in my head – but only in my head. It had the effect of reducing me to the same kind of childish stubbornness that he was using. I could think of nothing better to do than to lie down, shut my eyes and determine not to move or speak while they remained in the room.

About ten minutes passed with no sound but the rustle of the pages they were turning, and it occurred to me that if I moved into a more comfortable position and deliberately relaxed my muscles I could go to sleep, and *that* would show him! I am good at going to sleep in moments of stress, it's the defence which comes most naturally to me. So I curled into a sleeping position and was pleased to discover that it was going to work – another minute or so and I'd be off. I was almost disappointed when he saw what I was up to and admitted defeat. 'All right,' he said, 'I can see that you're tired. We'll leave you to sleep some more and see you later.' I buried a grin of triumph in the pillow, and went to sleep as soon as they were out of the door.

When I woke up again it was almost three o'clock and I was feeling better. I would get up now, I thought – and do my washing, because that, too, would show him. If he was waiting for me in my sitting-room (and I knew he was, I could feel him there), let him understand that I wasn't waiting for him.

They heard me in the bathroom and Halé came in to ask if I wanted anything to eat. That was a reasonable question, and since Hakim left me alone apart from calling out 'Hi!', I began to feel less cornered by them. An hour later, my chores finished, I thought it likely that they had now been converted back into ordinary guests so that I could join them in the sitting-room without discomfort.

A very few minutes proved me to be over-optimistic. Hakim had been able to restrain himself from dragging me away from the wash-bowl, but he was bubbling with impatience because this, as it turned out, was to be the day on which he would bring me to see the light.

The first warning was his appearance. He was sitting even stiller than usual and his expression was fixed, his lips drawn back in what would have been a smile if his eyes hadn't been so feverishly intense. Those extraordinary eyes were to be fixed on my face almost without interruption for the next eight or nine hours. The second warning was his return to the theme of 'I understand!' This time he was prepared to divulge what he understood.

It was the pitiful inadequacy of my life; it was that I felt myself to be advancing into old age as a failure; it was that I had no confidence in my own attractiveness or abilities. I recognised as he spoke that he was doing what he had done before: building a dotty structure on a grain of truth. The fantasy of my taking over Halé's body had been based on two such grains: he had picked up first my disappointment at his not arriving alone, which had been in fact strong enough for me to want to hide it, even though it was nowhere near so strong as he imagined; and he had picked up second the odd extent to which I was identifying with Halé's grief. His fantasy had run wild but it had not been wholly without content. And now he was picking up another truth about me. It happens that my self-confidence, particularly my sexual self-confidence, took a bad beating at one time and had since been repaired rather than restored. It became quite strong again, but like some damaged limb it had shrunk a bit. I had settled for not expecting certain things, so as not to be thrown when I didn't get them. This cautious, pain-avoiding habit of feeling seemed to me a serviceable one for a woman of my age and I certainly didn't want to be cured of it (indeed, it represents 'cure' in itself), but I was not proud of it and usually tried to conceal it. Although I could see that Hakim was going to make some kind of wild nonsense out of his perception, I had to grant that it was a perception.

His theme this afternoon was that if only I would trust him he would free me to make the bolder claims on life which I ought to be making. All I need do was to confess. I must understand that I needn't be ashamed or afraid before him; I could tell him anything bad I had ever done or thought of doing, and he would free me of my guilt about it so that I would no longer be crippled. He was going to do for me what he had done for Jean: 'cure' me.

What sort of thing, I asked him, did he expect me to come up with? Anything which I'd hitherto felt was too wicked or too embarrassing to confess. But how could I do that, when nothing seemed to me too wicked or embarrassing? Surely he must realise, I said, what a glutton I am for discussing my own and everyone else's behaviour? Surely he must know that even if I'd *murdered* someone it wouldn't seem 'unspeakable' to me (I'd have written a book about it by now!).

This response infuriated him, as though I were spoiling a carefully prepared script by improvising. I was lying; I was dodging. I must listen to him: and he began to throw me cues. My brother, for instance – hadn't I ever wanted to sneak into bed with my brother? My father – hadn't I ever spied on him through the bathroom key-hole? My nurse – hadn't I ever enjoyed her touching my genitals when she was bathing me?

'But Hakim,' I told him, 'If anything of that sort had happened in my childhood – I don't remember anything of that sort, but if it *had* happened, I'd *love* to tell you about it. It simply isn't the kind of thing which makes me feel ashamed. Infantile sex – any sex – doesn't seem any more shameful to me than it does to you.'

'But it *is* shameful – to children it is,' he said angrily. '*All* children feel it's shameful, so you must have done. Do you think I didn't find it shameful when once I let a man fuck me? Do you think I have ever been able to talk about *that*?'

That child growing up wild in a slum, listening to the bed creak when his father brought home his weekend women (he'd told me that); watching his sister get pregnant in her teens; fucking his first girl when he was about twelve – where had he got his guilt from? I suddenly remembered his explanation of why he always pulled the lavatory plug before he peed instead of afterwards – I'd noticed it and asked him about it, and he'd laughed when he told me that he didn't realise that he still did it, but Blondie, his father, had beaten him and his brother if they didn't do it, saying he would teach them manners because 'who wants to listen to people peeing'. Disorderly, not free, behaviour: that's what he'd felt he was surrounded by as a child. That's what his father had felt. Nice folks (folks with money, white folks) didn't behave as they did. Nice folks didn't make noises in the john, or fuck around, weren't crude or violent. What a fearful confusion of mind for a child to grow up surrounded by adults who constantly did all the things they beat their children for in the vague, intermittent hope that the children might become nearer to 'nice folks' than they were.

I couldn't say any of that to him. I could only say, 'But Hakim, love – now you *have* talked about letting a man fuck you, so you can see you were mistaken. It may have been horrible, but it's not *unspeakable*, is it?'

It didn't work. No attempt to turn the talk into straight discussion got through to him. I tried to give him something out of my own past on which genuinely to work. I dredged up a childhood dream about killing my brother by piercing his anus with a sword (one could hardly do better than that!), and another later dream about making love with a woman, but he didn't want to hear anything I was prepared to tell. I saw that I was supposed to be afraid. I must tremble, I must cry, I must blurt something out: that was what he was working for, and that was a performance that I certainly was not going to put on for him.

Somewhere in this absurd session I even began to feel uncomfortable at not being able to produce any genuine guilt or fear. It did seem dreadfully smug, if not improbable, to be so unmixed up. I searched my mind diligently, less for his sake than for my own: suppose it *was* only the thick crust of a good English upbringing which made me feel that I was unafraid and unguilty, while really, if only I dared face it, there were terrors seething underneath? I could hardly deny that the crust of my good English upbringing *was* very thick... I was letting him hassle me into involvement, and had to check myself.

Although he was hopelessly obtuse about argument – simply not open to it – he was uncannily alert to my reactions as I sat there opposite him. He sensed it at once if I was more annoyed at something he said than I pretended to be, or if I was refusing to admit that he had touched a nerve. And I on my side was as uncomfortably alert to him. I always knew where he was going to come at me before he pounced, and as the evening wore on I moved further and further away from a plain attempt to bring him down to talking sense, and nearer and nearer to fencing with him on his own terms.

From time to time I would say to myself, 'Oh Christ, this is getting boring – why don't I just get up and stomp out of the room?' But the truth was, I wasn't bored. Exhausted, yes; but not bored. There was no real question of my walking out – I couldn't even take my eyes off his face. I knew that Halé was in the room all the time but I soon stopped being aware of her presence while his seemed to fill the room, the flat, my head. Although I now gulp at having to admit it, at the time I was astounded – almost awe-struck – at the extent of the power this lunatic was wielding over me. And on this day we smoked nothing.

'All right,' he said at one point, 'you don't have to agree yet. We've got time. I can easily go on all night.' At that I remembered reading an account of psycho-pathic excitement and of how a patient in its grip stops needing to eat or sleep. It was obvious that Hakim *could* go on all night. He had eaten nothing all day, brushing off one or two suggestions from Halé that she might make some food, and at midnight he was still humming with energy. As I remember it, he never went out of the room to pee, either, although I can't be quite positive about that.

What finally broke the pattern of this crazy dialogue was when he came – as I knew he would sooner or later – to the vanished money. We had come round again, for the I-don't-know-how-manyeth time, to a denial on my part (by this time quite shakily apologetic) that I had any neurotic troubles to be cured of. 'How can you claim that you aren't neurotic,' he said – and this was going to be it, I knew, I was tensed to jump out of my chair before he'd gone any further – 'How can you claim that you aren't neurotic when you've just been to all that stupid trouble to lie about the money you were going to give me? You didn't have to do that. I'd have understood.'

The reason why I didn't strike him was because he had calculated that I would, and would have counted it a triumph. I was across the room with my hand raised before that knowledge checked me. Instead I grabbed him by the shoulders and shook him, shouting 'You bloody fool! Can't you *see* that if you want me to think you're infallible the last thing to do is to accuse me of something *I know I haven't done*? All that makes me do is see that you're a fool – a bloody *fool*!'

'Then why does it make you so mad?' he said, smirking.

'Because it's so fucking stupid,' I replied – knowing that in spite of his answer I had disconcerted him, and that the movement, the shouting, had broken the spell. It was very sudden – unexpected – but from that moment I knew that I was in control.

This was true. He tried to continue, but almost at once he gave me my opening. I can't remember what he said, but it enabled me to answer: 'Hakim, the whole point of this endless carry-on is to get me to admit that you know everything because you're God, isn't it?'

'Of course it is,' he said.

'And that,' I said, 'I am never going to do, because you are not.'

'It's for your sake,' he said. 'I don't mind, it doesn't matter to me if you believe it or not because your belief makes no difference to the truth.'

'If you feel like that, why are you taking all this trouble?'

'Because I love you. I want you to know.'

It was nearly over. He began staring at the floor instead of into my eyes, and his expression became very sad. I found my voice becoming gentle as I spoke to him – the voice of someone soothing a sick creature. Then at last I stood up and said, 'Look, love, you'll just have to accept that we must agree to differ, and now I'm going to bed.' He said nothing, just went on staring sadly at the floor. I went over to him and kissed his forehead before I left the room – he had become pathetic to me – and he didn't move or look up. I went to bed feeling ill with fatigue (next morning I weighed myself and found that in those two days wrestling with him I'd lost five pounds!), but I was confident that from now on he would leave me alone. Halé was to record that session in her diary almost as briefly as she had recorded the last one: 'We stayed in and talked all day. Diana is unable to believe that Hakim is God. It is strange how people refuse the light when it's offered to them.'

On the Monday morning they were both subdued. I woke them early and told them to drive me to the office by way of the bank. Hakim came with me into the bank. I cashed a cheque for £200, had it put in an envelope, slapped it into his hand and went briskly out to the car without letting him speak. For the rest of the drive I allowed nothing to be said but trivialities. When we reached the office he got out to escort me across the street to the door, and tried to put his arm round my shoulders, but I dodged it. 'What time will you be home this evening?' he asked, and looked dismayed when I told him that I would be out. I could in fact have come home early from that evening's engagement if I'd wanted to, but I meant to let it keep me as late as possible. Having delivered the money because I'd been fool enough to promise it, I was thankful to discover that I now felt quite unhooked from Hakim.

I thought during that day that I must establish when they were going to leave (nothing had been said about the length of their stay), but when I next saw them, on the evening of the following day, I saw that it would be unnecessary. Hakim's mood had changed completely and he wasn't going to push me beyond what was reasonable: I could bet on their leaving before a week was out. For the rest of their visit, in fact, our relationship was not disagreeable, although the friendliness was more superficial than it had been. We spent only one whole evening together. The rest of the time we saw each other only in passing, before they or I went out somewhere, or after we had come back. It was on one of the evenings when they were out and I wasn't that I looked at Halé's diary – a large copy-book with the written pages folded neatly back on themselves so that she could tell at a glance where she had got to. She left it about quite cheerfully because it was a record of what they had done, not of her thoughts or feelings.

On our evening together we struck a vein of pleasantly companionable talk. Halé was speculating on how she would get on with Hakim's family and old friends when she met them in the States, saying how odd it would be to meet for the first time people about whom she knew so much. This launched him on anecdotes about these people, some of them very amusing, and we started to swap strange characters we had known. It was so different from the weekend that he might have been a different person.

At nine o'clock the telephone rang and he said, 'Hell! That's Libbie – I can tell her ring by now. Look, one of you answer and say I'm not in yet.'

Libbie was one of the girls he'd laid on his first visit to me, the one who had fallen wildly in love with him. She was the clever, indulged child of a loving and well-off family with left-wing views, hard put to it to find anything to rebel against but trying her best, unhappy only because she was too fat and thought herself unattractive. To be pounced on by a beautiful black militant had been fulfilment of her dreams, and in the months since she'd first met Hakim she had been assiduously running errands for him, sending him books and

89

press-cuttings, telephoning newspaper editors on his behalf and generally making herself useful so that she would have excuses to telephone him in Morocco. She was a girl who felt it her duty to be above jealousy and possessiveness, and she knew, anyway, that Hakim would be irritated if she displayed such feelings, so she had been making a brave effort to feel friendly towards Halé; but she had, nevertheless, managed to lunch alone with him, and at lunch – it now came out – he had promised to visit her at eight-thirty this evening.

She was not a girl to stand on her dignity. After that first call she rang every fifteen or twenty minutes, and soon she was making no attempt to hide the fact that she was crying. 'But you *must* talk to her,' I told Hakim. 'If you really aren't going to go, you must at least tell her – you can say that something important has cropped up.'

'But I *can't*,' said Hakim, wriggling down in his chair with hunched shoulders. 'Oh hell, why was I such a fool?'

'Yes, why were you such a fool?'

'She wanted it so much.'

I turned to Halé for support, and she agreed that it was too bad to leave the poor girl dangling like this. As she joined me in prodding him into action I got the impression that she was feeling slightly daring. Telling Hakim he was a fool! Saying that he was being feeble! We were all laughing (poor Libbie!) but it still seemed slightly blasphemous to Halé, I suspected.

At last, when it was almost midnight, he decided that he hadn't the nerve to tell the unhappy girl that he wasn't coming, so if neither Halé nor I would act as intermediary he would have to go. But she lived in some remote suburb, so how would he get there? His car had finally collapsed and he was unaccustomed to driving on the left so he didn't want to take mine – he never drove himself in London if he could help it. But Halé could drive him in my car, if I wasn't going to need it early in the morning. 'We wouldn't be late back.' I said that turning up with Halé would be worse than not turning up at all: imagine this infatuated, tear-bedaubed girl having to welcome his woman when all she wanted was him! Halé agreed that it would be hard on her. 'OK,' said Hakim, 'Halé can drop me and come straight back – we'll see how it works out.' Meanwhile I was to call Libbie and tell her that he was on his way, inventing some reason why the message had to come through me and not from him.

Off they went and I called Libbie. Her quivering gasp of joy made me blush for the flippancy with which we'd been discussing her. I didn't tell her that Halé would be with him, although I was certain that Hakim would get his way and that she would not be back that night.

I didn't see them again until the following evening, and in the intervening time Libbie called me with a message about something she was doing for Hakim, almost singing with happiness. 'By the sound of that girl's voice,' I said when he came in, 'you must have given her a marvellous time.' 'Marvellous,' he said smugly; and Halé added 'Just think what she'd have sounded like if he hadn't gone after all!' There was a shade of reproof in her voice, as though it had been I, not Hakim, who had nearly deprived Libbie of her bliss. I asked Halé where she had slept. In Libbie's sitting-room, she said, and her cheerful serenity could not have sounded less forced. She felt, or so it seemed to me, that when Hakim chose to go to bed with another woman he was not making love to her so much as *bestowing his blessing* on her: something which it would be unthink-able to grudge. And Hakim almost certainly felt the same.

A couple of days later they did something much less benevolent, this time to the husband of the woman who had offended Hakim by saying that he trembled for love of her. Hakim told me more than once that he intended to inform this man that he had slept with his wife, putting him wise to the kind of bitch she was. Each time I'd answered that this was a disgusting suggestion. Asked why he wanted to do it, he came out with self-righteous statements about being unable to deceive a man he liked – 'He's a sweet guy and I hate to see him taken by that bitch' – and pompous declarations that he was compelled to tell the truth about everything because that was his nature. That, I had pointed out with all the energy at my command, is the classic rationalisation of the destructively aggressive person who is itching to give pain but won't admit it. He had seemed to give way, but the subject obviously excited him: it brought his fixed smile to his face and an extra alertness into his manner, and I could see that if he met the man again he wouldn't be able to resist the scene. The only hope was that other things would distract him so that he wouldn't seek his victim out.

However, he came home one evening looking specially bright-eyed and announced: 'We went to see Z this afternoon.'

'You didn't tell him?'

'Of course I did – I had to.'

'Hakim told him everything,' said Halé, who was also looking jubilant – she loathed the couple because they disliked her.

'That was a disgusting thing to do,' I said, but neither of them took the slightest notice; and curiosity made me stay in the room and ask what had happened.

'He told me to leave and said that I would no longer be welcome in his house.'

Quoting these words, Hakim assumed a self-satisfied expression as though they were just what he had been expecting, or even playing for, but I felt that he was disguising a trace of discomfort and that the husband had probably handled this repulsive situation with enough sense and dignity to make him aware, if only for a second, of the figure he was cutting. If so, however, he was soon able to gloss it over and become high again on a dual pleasure: that of being so honest that he would rather lose a friend than deceive him or see him deceived, and the far meatier one which he refused to admit: that of kicking a white man in the balls. Or perhaps of kicking *anyone* in the balls, once something about them had started to make them feel burdensome to him. Later I was to see that he was on the verge of doing something no less damaging to Charles Gooding, who was not only black but his oldest friend as well.

Surprisingly, I let him come to bed with me after all, on their last night. They came home late from a dinner-party given for them by an old friend of Halé's, which had ended disastrously. Halé was silent and downcast; Hakim in a state of obvious distress.

He had started the evening, he said, with the best of intentions; there was to be no argument, no hostility, nothing but kindness and enjoyment, so he'd complimented everyone on everything – their clothes, their looks, the food. 'I was nothing but *kind*.' But after dinner a girl sitting on the floor at his feet had started to talk about the astonishing physical change in Halé – how slim she was now, when she used to be so fat – and said that she would give anything for the same thing to happen to her.

'I only wanted to help her... Now listen, is this so terrible, was this such a bad thing to do? I said to her: 'Tell me, have I ever lied to you?' and she said no. So I said 'Do you think I'm going to lie to you now?', and she said no...'

'Oh Hakim, love,' I broke in, 'you told her you were God!'

'Yes I did,' he said miserably. 'I wanted to help her so that she could get slim. I don't see what was *bad* about that.'

'But you *must* know by now how it rattles people when you say that you're God!'

'They weren't rattled,' interjected Halé in a furious voice. 'They were *vicious*.'

Hakim said that they had gone at him 'with real hatred' and that it had been horrible. One man hadn't been so bad – he'd been prepared to argue, and when he'd finally said that he couldn't grant that Hakim was God because he was an atheist, Hakim could accept that. But another man had been angry and cruel, and 'if Halé hadn't gone and fetched our coats so that we could leave, I don't know what would have happened.'

He sat huddled in his chair, his hands trembling. I hadn't seen him so tense and unhappy since the last night of his first visit to me, when he was afraid of returning to the US. As it had done then, his disarray stimulated my mothering juices, and I felt moved to do whatever I could to 'make it better'. Halé appeared to think that she couldn't be much use. She took out her scrap-books, in which she kept cuttings about Hakim, articles by him, and photographs, and began quietly to insert the latest batch, sitting in her usual cross-legged position on the floor. I made tea and got to work on him, determined to coax him into laughing and relaxing, and soon he began to listen and respond, looking altogether better, so that I reckoned I could say goodnight – or rather, goodbye, because they had said that they were catching an early plane next day and might have to leave the flat before I was up.

I kissed first Halé, then Hakim. He held on to my hand after I had kissed him, letting it go very reluctantly, and I thought, Ha! He's back in the mood when he would like to come into my bed for comfort – the feeling's just the same. So although the opening of my bedroom door about half an hour later woke me up, it didn't surprise me. I knew it was him even before he said 'Brrr! It's cold in this room!'

'It's warm enough in bed,' I said, 'but turn on the heater if you like'; and only on speaking did I realise that I didn't mind if he got into bed with me.

He got quickly in, then propped himself on his elbow, looking down at me, and said, 'Do you *want* me to make love to you? I've been beginning to wonder.' He sounded genuinely uncertain – a tone which I never heard in his voice at any other time, which struck me as being strangely 'normal'.

When I say 'I didn't mind' I use the words deliberately; I had no particular wish to make love with him, but I thought it might be more agreeable than not: his unhappiness had caused a renewal of fondness for him, and tomorrow he'd be gone. Besides which, saying 'yes' rather than 'no' to love-making was the habit of a lifetime. Sleepily, I wanted him to understand my state of mind, so I said 'Yes, I think I'd like to make love. Look – it wouldn't *matter* if we didn't, but doing something nice is better than not doing it – that's what I feel.' I hoped this would 'un-God' him and reduce the occasion to an embrace of mundane sensuality between friends, free of transcendental implications. Halé's presence in the flat didn't worry me at all, now that I'd seen for myself how calmly she had taking his fucking Libbie when she was in attendance.

Perhaps I did manage to inhibit his God-feelings; this, the third of our love-makings, was less intense than the other two, which may have been because he wasn't getting the full thrill of believing that he was giving me something of inexpressible value. That, I am sure, was the stimulant to which he responded most keenly: the sense of himself as a bestower of bliss. And I, of course, was more detached than I had been. I remember trying an experiment. At a moment when his head was on my breast and our position was one to heighten the maternal element in my response, I thought, I wonder how he'd take it if I said 'child' to him? So I kissed his eyes softly and whispered 'Darling child'. There was an instant of stillness as though, disconcerted, he had caught his breath, and then he simply gave the words back to me. Equally softly, but with no expression, he said 'Darling child', and I knew that God hadn't cared for the endearment. He stayed with me for an hour, then returned to Halé after an affectionate and gentle goodnight.

Next morning I saw nothing of him but the top of his head sticking out of the bedclothes spread on the floor (they were sleeping on mattresses in the sitting-room for some reason – I suppose the spare-room must have been made up for someone else, although I can't remember anyone in it at the time). Halé was up and dressed, finishing their packing. I squatted down, pulled the blanket back and inch or two and kissed a corner of his forehead. He wriggled a hand out, caught my hand and pulled it under the covers to give it a long kiss. And that, looking back on it, was the last trace of the affectionate intimacy which had existed between us during his earlier visits and which had made a brief and subdued reappearance the night before.

It was another false departure. Their preparations and what they had said had suggested that they were off to catch a plane to the United States that morning, but they didn't do so. A week later I learnt by chance that Halé was still in London and that Hakim had gone back to Paris. Libbie learnt it too, and telephoned me half in tears and half angry: 'What's the point of all these lies? It's so humiliating.' To me it seemed that there was no point. It was just that Hakim felt no commitment to relationships – they existed only while they stimulated him, or were useful. Jean had written him a couple of fond letters and these – he told me much later – had decided him to have another go at her. I had the impression that while he'd been in Paris the first time, having this sick woman to play with had been exciting enough to eclipse the 'business' side of his invasion of her life, but he had still got some money out of her. She had cabled $200 to Dorothy and the £40 Hakim and Halé had on them when they arrived in London must have come from her (or from Romain Gary?). Now her letters must have persuaded him that he hadn't ploughed that furrow to the end. What happened during this second sortie I never learnt. Three weeks later he picked Halé up at London airport and they went on together to the USA – probably (this is only a guess) with more cash in their pockets than they would have had if he hadn't seen Jean again.

Nine

Almost a year later I was in New York on my way home from the West Indies, and heard from Hakim's publisher that Hakim was around. I said to give him my telephone number if he showed up within the next week, and heard from him next day. We arranged that he should come to my hotel at twelve-thirty on the last day of my trip.

He arrived alone, which didn't surprise me because some time in the intervening months he'd written to tell me that Halé had left him. 'It's been too much for her,' he had said, without giving details. Now, when we went to a nearby drugstore for coffee and sandwiches, I postponed asking what had happened because I thought he would tell more if he came to it of his own accord. He said that 'a friend' would be calling for him at two-thirty, driving his old VW bus, and I soon began to suspect that 'a friend' was Halé. He referred to her in a way which showed that they were still together, saying that their months in the States had been hard on her, she had become nervous and scared. 'She started crying a lot.'

'Scared of *you*?' I asked, and he answered 'Yes.' But I was not sure – and am still not sure – that he had heard me correctly, because the drugstore was full of music and voices. He had seen, he said, that she must have 'a rest-cure', so he had sent her off to Ohio to collect the VW which had been stranded there for a long time after a breakdown. There was no 'God talk', only a great deal about how unbearable and frightening the USA was, and he would have seemed sane if he hadn't suddenly insisted on talking French in order to 'fool' the girl serving us and his neighbour on the other side, a black woman, into thinking he was a foreigner. It was something, he said, which he and Halé often did to avoid the hostile reaction they would otherwise have met with.

I could understand this, having observed the stony eyes suddenly turned on me by the hitherto courteous people in my hotel after they had seen our embrace on meeting, but the way he did it was so exhibitionist and clumsy that it was far from serving its purpose. There had been no hostility at the counter when we first sat down and were talking English, but as soon as he embarked on his French act people started looking at him with suspicion. He seemed to be unaware of this.

Back at my hotel, he came up to talk to me while I finished packing (more poisonous looks), and reverted to a relaxed and normal manner as soon as we were alone. And when we came down with my luggage it was, as I'd expected, Halé who was waiting outside in the VW. I thought of asking him why he'd described her as 'a friend', but couldn't be bothered.

They offered to drive me to the airport after giving me a conducted tour of 'their' New York – the East Village, where they had been sleeping on a variety of floors and where the bus had been broken into three times. Jean's white sheepskin coat had gone, and so had an old Afghan coat I'd given Hakim, his typewriter and his tape-recorder (both new since Morocco). I asked why they hadn't taken their stuff indoors with them, and they said that the kind of pads they were staying in seemed more risky than the car. In spite of the broken windows, however, the car was cosy. Halé had made pretty curtains for its windows, and they had fixed up the back with foam rubber and shelves so that it was comfortable to live in.

They were both eager to demonstrate how horrible New York was, pointing out every junkie and every down-and-out we passed. In retaliation I started pointing out anything pleasant I noticed – a woman and child laughing together, the red and gold pagoda roofs on the telephone booths in Chinatown – but it was true that being in that scary city with people who had no money *did* sharpen my eye to its decay and cruelty, and it was impossible not to marvel at Halé's courage. When she wanted to pee we had to circle back to my hotel so that she could use my bathroom (I'd payed for that day so that I needn't be out by lunchtime). Eating, washing, peeing, sleeping – all the ordinary things of life were, and had been for months, things to be contrived; and contrived against more than indifference. It would have terrified me to live like that, even with a white man, while with Hakim… 'You can't believe what it's been like,' said Halé. 'That terrible *look* wherever we go, even if there's nothing worse.' Her excursion to Ohio to fetch the car – her 'rest-cure' – had been as frightening as the rest of it. She hadn't known whether the people he'd left the car with would give it up to her, and they'd been rude and suspicious; she'd run out of money and had been forced to let garage attendants feel her up when she needed gas. She said she knew now what being frightened was like. She obviously felt it a valuable lesson, and was proud to be learning it: millions of black people had to live like this, so it was only right that she should learn it from the inside. 'You know, Diana, I'll have to write about it soon,' she said, 'I really *have* been having an unusual experience.' And that was true. She was there because of a crazy infatuation – because some vacuum in her needed filling with an emotion of sacrifice and self-immolation – but she *was* there, and she was doing her best to bring back evidence. A trivial thing which particularly struck me was that she, as well as Hakim, was smelling quite strongly of sweat – stale sweat: something so foreign to the physical fastidiousness and elegance they shared that it drove home their outlawed condition with considerable force.

But they were cheerful that afternoon, full of laughter and talk and of nostalgia for London and the days they'd spent in my clean and peaceful flat. We got on well, and at the airport we even became hilarious. My firm had a special relationship with the air-line I was flying with, in connection with a book we were publishing, and without my knowing it my partner had alerted them to look out for me. Just as I was getting into trouble at the weighing-in counter because my baggage, during my holiday, had become overweight, an elegant official swooped in to identify and rescue me, and invited me to go and wait in the first-class lounge although I was travelling economy class. We were conducted through with considerable ceremony. By that time my hand-luggage had become slummy-looking, and both Hakim and Halé looked downright disreputable (the more so for their dramatic handsomeness), and we all became giggly as though we were carrying off some daring fraud. (Secretly, too, I felt extra amusement at Hakim's evident respect, under his laughter, for this indication of 'his' publisher's import-ance.) We spent a childishly happy half-hour in our unexpected luxury, and parted with hugs and kisses.

But when, some three months later, he wrote to say that they were heading for London again, I found that cau-tion had become stronger than hospitality. I wanted no more of Hakim's God-bullying, and the 'vanished' money reappeared in my mind: I realised that I now believed that Halé had taken it and that Hakim knew she had done so. There was no danger of their taking any more – I'd be careful from now on – but their predatory aspect could no longer be overlooked, particularly as my phone bill after their last visit indicated that they must often have called the USA without telling me.

I told them they were welcome to come to the flat for two or three days while they were looking for somewhere else to stay, but that was all, and I said why, explaining that last time he'd leant on me too heavily, and that anyway it was someone else's turn to pay for their phone calls. And when it turned out that this time there were three of them, because they had Charles Gooding in tow, I was thankful that I'd made this stand in advance.

At first sight Charles looked as though he would be boring to have around. He was a short, slight, sickly-looking man. He had lost his teeth which made his face look smaller than it ought to be even when he wore his dentures (usually he didn't, Halé told me, but now he was on his best behaviour). Hakim, because of his proportions and handsomeness, could make cheap and uninteresting clothes look stylish, but on Charlie they were drab. He looked like someone who might have come to deliver a parcel or read the gas-meter.

My first reaction to him, in fact, was a class reaction, and this shocked me. I was seeing him *de haut en bas*, as I had never seen Hakim or other people I knew from the same kind of background who happened not to be labelled by a certain kind of physical appearance. It was to *an appearance* that I was responding by feeling bored (we will have nothing in common) and condescending (I must try to put the poor little man at his ease), even enunciating with special care and avoiding long words as though his lack of education meant he was simple-minded (later I noticed other people doing this when they first met him). Because I was ashamed of my reaction I mustered all my skill to disguise it; and since my social skills are well developed I succeeded well enough not to put Charlie off. As a result he was soon able to dispel my boredom and condescension – but not during the first evening when he hardly spoke and was being explained behind his back, during escapes into the kitchen and so on, by Hakim and Halé.

He and Hakim had known each other since they were small boys, but Charlie had stayed 'on the corner' as a drunk while Hakim had left Boston and launched on his new life. When he and Halé had gone to visit his boyhood haunts, a month or so earlier, they had found Charlie much as he had always been, and drunk, but delighted to see his old friend. Hakim had pounced on him and had started drying him out. 'Be gentle with him,' said Hakim. 'He's never much of a talker and now he's feeling very shaky because he hasn't had a drink for three weeks after thirty-five years being pickled in the stuff.' They had brought him to England with them because they were both committed to giving him full support – and they were, indeed, surrounding him with an affectionate attention which clearly meant a lot to him. He had fallen in love with Halé, Hakim said; but if he had it was a humble and unaspiring love because his relationship with Hakim was evidently that of a follower, not a rival.

How the three of them had been able to afford to cross the Atlantic and to bring the VW bus with them I didn't ask – it wasn't a question likely to get a truthful answer. The back of the bus was even better equipped than before because Charlie, a handy man who earned a little money from time to time by doing jobs about people's houses, had contributed many refinements. In Boston Hakim and Halé had stayed at first with Hakim's mother, now a widow, but she had soon thrown them out and they'd moved on to park in Charlie's back yard (or rather, in his grandmother's, because he lived in her house). Hakim declared himself mystified by his mother's behaviour, speaking of it with pain as yet another chapter in the story of her rejection of him and casting her as the villain of the incident; but I knew him well enough by now to suspect that her version would have been different and probably more convincing.

I think – I don't *know* because simply by being there I would have altered the conditions – that when Hakim was with blacks, no whites present, he was far more effective than I ever saw him being. Charlie needed as badly as anyone to hear a message which would give him a sense of his own value and dignity, so he was ready to gobble up simplifications; but he was no fool, and Hakim managed to move him deeply. I never asked him to describe the exact circumstances of his decision to dry out because he was still in the thick of it and I felt it was something private and so important to him that no one should make him talk about it unless he wanted to; but I did hear from him in so many words that what Hakim had done for him, by shaking up his thoughts, was so valuable to him that he was prepared to put up with a lot of nonsense for its sake.

Because it hadn't been long before he'd become aware of the nonsense, and what he told me explained the 'over-excited' manner I'd noticed in Hakim. 'The only trouble is,' said Charlie, 'all his talk about being God. I wish he wouldn't do that.'

'Oh lord!' I said, 'Has he been on that kick a lot?'

'Has he been on it! He was on television to talk about his book, and he ended by telling the whole world he was God. All Boston was talking about it for days.' At first Charlie had thought that he didn't really mean it, 'but now I'm beginning to think he does.' It had been very embarrassing at times. On one occasion Charlie had gone with Hakim and Halé to some college campus where Hakim had been invited to address the students. They'd given him a good reception and he had spoken well, 'but he ended by getting kind of excited, you know how he does, and telling all these kids he was God – and they were bright kids, you know, middle-class kids with a good education, and they played along with him, kind of like a joke, and he didn't seem to see it, he thought they were serious.'

I asked him whether he thought Halé believed in Hakim's divinity, and he said he couldn't make her out. Sometimes she'd seem not to and would tell him to cool it, but at other times she seemed to believe. It had been worrying Charlie quite a lot. It worried me too, I told him, because soon we'd be publishing Hakim's book and we'd like to set up interviews for him and so on, in order to publicise it, but if he was going to use interviews as chances to announce his divinity he'd be written off as a nut and it would do more harm than good. Charlie thought that now he'd reached England he'd probably calm down; he hoped so, anyway. He might be a bit mad – well, he *was* a bit mad – but he was still 'brilliant'.

It was obviously a relief to Charlie to meet someone with whom he could discuss Hakim's madness without feeling treacherous – he knew that I, like him, didn't *want* his friend to make a fool of himself. I was careful not to try to get more out of him than he was prepared to give, and our talk stayed within a framework of concern and affection for Hakim. I was somewhat hypocritical in order to keep it within that framework, appearing to accept Charlie's assessment of Hakim's intellectual stature which I didn't really share. My own assessment would have been that he had an acute natural intelligence hampered by ignorance and increasingly confused by psychological disturbance; but I could see why he was 'brilliant' to Charlie. Who else in Roxbury had even thought of writing a book, still less got one accepted by publishers in New York and London? Who else had moved out into the world of white people – and *grand* white people such as film stars and publishers – with such apparently dashing assurance? I myself, and Charlie's presence in my London flat, were part of the proof of Hakim's 'brilliance.' And who else had been able to make Charlie really feel the importance of Malcolm X and his teaching? I felt that Charlie was on this jaunt for the fun of it, but that his involvement didn't stop there: he was also making a bid for regeneration, and this would depend a lot on his respect for Hakim, so I mustn't tamper with this respect.

But Hakim didn't calm down in England; instead he was interested in nothing but chances to tell people he was God, and in 'debating'. After three days they moved to a room in North Kensington, but to begin with they reappeared at my place several times for baths and food, and he was always eager to plunge into this fatuous logic-chopping with whoever was there. Halé would behave as though she were in privileged and enjoyable attendance on a great teacher ('I don't think you have understood what Hakim means,' she would say gently when someone tried to make him see how pointless his 'debating' was). Charlie knew that it was embarrassing. It made a better impression on uneducated black people, he once told me, than it did on educated whites; it wasn't always a mistake; but it *was* a pity that Hakim couldn't tell when it wasn't working. I would try to steer the talk towards the past, because it was only when Hakim was reminiscing that he made sense, or let Charlie do so. The most agreeable part of these occasions was when Charlie got going and Hakim sat back to allow him his head, looking as though he were exhibiting a successful achievement. But I doubted whether he'd have been so pleased if he'd known how freely Charlie talked in his absence, and I think Charlie shared that doubt: there was a shade of conspiracy in the way we didn't tell Hakim about our talks. It was in the air that Hakim had thought of 'fixing Charlie up' with me – he tended to leer if he left us together and to look at us sharply when he rejoined us, and he had certainly sold me to Charlie in a big way. But if Charlie knew this he had far too much sense and tact to betray it.

On one of the bath-visits Hakim spoke again about Michael Malik (or Michael de Freitas, or Michael X – the man who had been so disagreeable when we published his book) – I don't remember that we had referred to him during the interval since, at the start of our acquaintance, he'd asked me to introduce them and I had discouraged him. By now Michael had left England. There had been a brouhaha when he and his henchmen had forced a small sum of money (about £3) off a man who, they claimed, owed it to them, and had then dragged him round a room by what was described as a 'slave collar'. He had been charged with robbing the man, had jumped bail and had gone to his native Trinidad where, it seemed, the British police were glad to leave him. 'I was a fool,' Hakim said. 'I shouldn't have listened to what people said. I should have understood that it was a conspiracy to keep us apart.' I pretended not to see that he was suggesting that I was one of the conspirators, and asked why he was so interested in Michael. 'I have a strong feeling that he and I would have a lot in common,' he said. I left it at that, silently congratulating myself on having done my bit in preventing the meeting. I reckoned by now that they *did* have a lot in common: if they had come together it would surely have done Hakim even less good than I had suspected when he first raised the subject, and I was thankful that Michael was safely out of the country.

Early in this visit Hakim polished off his relationship with Libbie – and did it, by his own account, with considerable brutality. He had said that she was becoming a bore, and had kept sending him cables while he was in the States asking him to telephone her about something important, but when he did it would turn out that she just wanted to hear his voice. He quickly went to meet her, however, and she turned up 'with her little boyfriend'. They all had lunch together and

Hakim suddenly decided 'to tell her the truth about herself'. 'I was brutal,' he said. 'I had to be, for her own good, it was the only way to free her.' She had cried and 'that little boy – he jumped up and challenged me, he was a good little boy,' said Hakim condescendingly. His line was that he had engineered the scene so that Libbie would be cured of her obsession with him and would start to respect the boy, but this sounded to me like justification after the event. My hunch was that the scene had been triggered by the girl's daring to turn up with another man, and I remember thinking that if Charlie and I had felt like taking up the opportunity which Hakim supposed himself (I'm sure) to be 'giving' us, he'd soon have provided himself with a reason to punish us in some way.

Hakim was working on a new book, the story of his relationship with Jean. He had shown me the first two chapters earlier and I had advised him to go on with it because he seemed to be hitting off very well the way it had felt to him: half a great lark, half frightening because of the guilt involved and the tricky business of its getting more difficult to handle the more enjoyable it became. We agreed that he should bring me chapters as he finished them so that I could edit the grammar and so on, and no time would be wasted. It was obvious that the better the book turned out the more technically libellous it would be, so I warned him that we would be unlikely to be able to publish it; but Jean had told him that she wouldn't make trouble (for what that was worth—she was already suing two magazines for saying that he was the father of the dead baby) and he was confident that he would find a buyer for it in America. He wanted to finish it quickly so that he could use the money he got for it to finance a return to Morocco or a visit to some other part of Africa.

It was soon apparent that the book was going off the rails. Hakim's disorder was becoming increasingly apparent in his writing as well as in his behaviour. Earlier, writing about Malcolm X, he had given too much weight to slight incidents although without exaggerating the incidents themselves, and now he was doing the same thing only more so. Jean would ask him if he knew so-and-so and he would interpret it as an attempt to spy on the Panthers; she would wangle him an invitation to speak at a meeting on the problems of black people in Watts, there would be a few whites in the audience, and he would realise that he had been 'tricked' into 'giving himself away'. He interpreted as sinister the fact that one day, when he was with Jean, a photographer she knew turned up and said he'd heard that morning that Che Guevara was in Brazil. The man had heard it on the radio, but in Hakim's mind it was converted into proof that Jean commanded secret knowledge. She was a spy.

Whom, I asked, would she be spying for? The American government – or the British... or perhaps the French. Who could tell? Her husband put her up to it. But what, I asked, would be the use to any government of the kind of information which, by his own account, she was angling for, if that had been what she was doing? It was only the names of organisations, or whether someone was a Panther: stuff easily available from the local police, if not from the press. This argument flustered him and made him angry.

Reading between the lines it seemed possible that in one sense Jean *had* been 'using' him – and her husband, who was to write a novel based on Jean's relationship with Hakim, may have been doing so too: some kind of voyeurish complicity between husband and wife was indicated here and there. For all the naturalness of her letters to him, she could at some level have been using him as experience and as fuel for her need to demonstrate her lack of racism; to exercise virtue and to acquire merit. What white can plead total innocence of such using in relationships with blacks, at least at some point? And this Hollywood-conditioned girl might be extra self-deceiving. Such merit was fashionable in her circle, at that time; hard to resist, no doubt. To be the one who *really* knew about what went on in the ghettos, the one who *really understood* what black people feel – she may have wanted that pre-eminence. It would be characteristic of Hakim to smell a falseness quickly, if falseness was there, and equally characteristic of him to turn what he had sensed into something fanciful and crude, such as 'spying' or 'treachery'. That, I guessed, was how it had gone.

To start with I tried to weed out the paranoia and save the factual story, which remained a good one, but his text became increasingly wild until I saw that I couldn't do it. Either I had to go on sub-editing a load of nonsense, or I had to stop. I stopped.

The last straw was hearing that Hakim was talking about me (more, apparently, in sorrow than in anger) as a traitor: I and my colleagues had taken on his book in order to suppress his ideas and were doing our best not to sell it. Here again he was running true to form: the accusation was absurd but it had grown out of a seed of truth. The book had been taken on partly to humour me, in the certain knowledge that we could sell only a small printing of it. Only a tiny part of the British public cares two pins about black people in America or anywhere else, and even that part easily becomes fatigued at the prospect of being made to feel more guilty than it feels already. Even if we made strenuous efforts to push the book we would achieve no more than making a small sale slightly less small, so we were making only mediocre efforts; and things which we would have done gladly because they cost nothing, such as setting up interviews with gossip columnists and persuading television producers that the author would be good value on the screen, we were deliberately not doing because we knew that Hakim would destroy the value of such free publicity by ranting about being God. (Angered by our inertia, Halé had taken over as Hakim's 'promoter', and managed to get him some publicity of this sort, whereupon he did exactly what I expected and was written off as a nut.) To make matters worse the woman then in charge of our publicity disliked him on sight and thought we were crazy to have taken him on, which of course he spotted at once. But in spite of all this our publication of the book had *not* been an elaborate plot to bottle his ideas between book covers and keep them hidden in our warehouse; nor had he been deceived about the book's prospects. I had warned him repeatedly that he must not expect too much from publication in England – if we sold 2000 copies we would be lucky – and I had begged him in writing as well as face to face to control his urge to proclaim his divinity, for the book's sake. His version of events therefore made me angry, and it pointed to trouble if I went on working on his new book. If I was to aim at making it publishable I must modify its lunacies; and if I modified its lunacies he would soon start accusing me of perverting his ideas.

Since he had started complaining about me behind my back he had not come to see me, either out of disgust or because he was reluctant to be nasty to me in person. I decided, therefore, to drive over to the house in North Kensington where they were staying and leave the typescript for him with a letter explaining why I was pulling out.

I couldn't continue with the job, I wrote, unless I cut out the madness; and the way he'd started going on about me behind my back made it clear how he'd react if I did that. Crossly, I added that when I did something like editing a man's script for free regardless of who, eventually, would publish it, I did it not out of any sense of obligation but simply for fun; so if it stopped being fun – *finito!*

They were all out when I arrived at the house (and their host, who had been a devoted fan of Hakim's, could hardly bring himself to speak his name or to take in the parcel – there was evidently trouble brewing there, though what it was I never learnt). Three hours later Hakim, very agitated, arrived at my flat.

He didn't mind my giving up work on the book, he said: that was fair enough, if I didn't feel like doing it I shouldn't, and he approved of my honesty. But was I going to stop being his friend because I thought he was mad?

Hadn't he stopped being my friend? I countered.

No, of course he hadn't. All right, he might sometimes *say* things, but he didn't mean them. And if I stopped loving him because he was mad, that would be horribly unfair. Perhaps I was right – how could he tell? – but if I was, what could he do about it? He was what he was, and he couldn't change.

His voice began to pound at me. Sometimes he became incoherent, but his main gist was clear enough. His expression was that of a man with a bitter taste in his mouth, and his eyes stared into space, not into mine – he wasn't trying to dominate. He knew, he said, exactly what I thought of him – I and other white people. Here, we said, was an emotional, unstable black man with no education and a painful background, probably rather primitive in his reactions, and things had happened to him which he couldn't cope with. Malcolm X had saved him from the gutter and had filled his life with love – the only love he'd ever known – and when Malcolm was killed, all his hope had been snatched away and he had cracked under the strain. So look what had happened (this was still supposed to be me, or someone like me, speaking): he had suffered what was called a brainstorm and came out of it believing that Malcolm's soul had entered his body. He had started wearing Malcolm's hat, and glasses just like Malcolm's, even though he didn't need glasses. And after that – well, obviously a man capable of believing that another man's soul possessed his body would have no trouble in going a step further and believing he was God. A paranoid delusion: yes, he knew what people thought and said, and that I was now thinking the same. Poor, mad Hakim, thrown by events which had been too much for him! He knew I saw him like that, but he knew even more strongly that I was wrong. Or he *felt* that he knew I was wrong. Or perhaps I wasn't wrong – perhaps he *was* mad. But surely I could see that it was impossible for him to change, even if he was? Would I have to withdraw my friendship? He couldn't bear it if I did.

The room wasn't cold but he'd kept on his coat, with the collar turned up, and although as usual he sat quite still while his voice raced on, he was huddled rather than relaxed. He repeated himself a lot, was sometimes more coherent, sometimes less so. Every now and then his voice rose to a hectoring shout, but he never looked at me, not even when he was making a direct appeal: 'Don't *you* try to change me, let me be mad if that's what I am, don't stop being my friend.'

I was surprised to discover that I was not painfully moved; I was simply waiting for him to come to the end of it, and go. The word 'bored' would be wrong: there was a weight of sadness on me, a grief that wouldn't have been present in simple boredom. But the sense that Hakim was going to get worse, not better, and that it was useless to think of him as a person with whom I could communicate rationally, was very oppressive. It was poignant that he should be making these admissions about himself in what he took to be my voice, and should be getting it so right, but it didn't have the effect I would have expected. I would have expected to feel 'But he's getting down to the truth! If he can see this much, then perhaps he may be able to see further and get rid of his madness altogether!' With surprise I observed that this feeling was entirely absent. Instead of hope, I felt that his condition was all the sadder for him to endure and for me to witness because it had these glimmerings of awareness mixed up in it. Surely someone mad must be better off if he can exist wholly within his madness, never seeing it from the outside.

'Of course I'm still your friend,' I said, and at last went over to kiss his forehead and hold his hand, soothing him as I had done when he had occasional fits of ranting during his earlier visits, but feeling sure that now he was beyond real soothing. He went through the motions of accepting reassurance, but his expression didn't change. He stood up and we went out into my hall, still hand in hand, and there he halted and stood motionless, staring straight ahead as though at his own thoughts. I buttoned up his coat and turned down his collar, 'mothering' him. Without looking at me he said: 'I'm crazy about you, you know. It's been very difficult with Halé and Charlie around all the time, but I'll get away soon, and come round and we'll have a sweet evening together. I'll make love to you.'–'You do that darling,' I said. 'I'll look forward to it.' I knew for sure that he wouldn't come – none of his usual energy was coming off him. We were pretending – simply exchanging tokens of affection to comfort ourselves for the fact that I wanted to be rid of him.

A friend of Halé's gave a little party to celebrate the publication of *From the Dead Level* . Halé didn't want to invite me, because she thought that my firm should have been giving him a big one, and I didn't want to go, but I couldn't tell Hakim that. I did, however, tell him that I would have to leave early because of some tiresome (and non-existent) business commitment. I was sure he would make a great fool of himself at it, and I couldn't bear to watch him doing so.

When I arrived he was enthroned on a chair in the centre of the room, with Halé to one side of him, on a sofa, surrounded by bits of paper and a tape-recorder, and the rest of the guests in a rough circle around him, on chairs or the floor, looking embarrassed or bored. I went over to sit by Charlie, hoping for some gossip, but soon realised that we weren't supposed to be speaking to each other: we were there as an audience. Hakim had his 'prick-eared' look and his fixed grin, and was saying nothing: it was Halé's job to 'present' him.

She began by reading an article he'd once written about his childhood. It was rather good, as most of his communications about his 'pre-Malcolm' days were. Then she apologised because she had not been able to get the tape of a broadcast interview in which he'd explained that he was God. Instead she would...I can't remember what it was that she proposed, but it didn't meet with Hakim's approval. He yelled at her. His words were disagreeable enough – something like, 'Shut your mouth and do as you are told' – but the brutality of his manner was worse, jolting the whole room. Everyone looked away from Halé, to spare her, but when after a second or two I looked at her again she was smiling sweetly with what appeared to be unforced serenity.

At that point I stood up and said that alas, I had to go. Hakim rose too, and embraced me as I said the usual kind of congratulatory and luck-wishing words, and I asked him to sign a copy of his book which I had brought with me. He came out into the hall with me and wrote his inscription with the book propped against the wall, then handed it to me and watched with grinning defiance as I read it. 'Time alone will tell all of "them" are guilty of something – not me – I tell the truth because, I AM GOD!!! THERE IS NONE LIKE ME. Jamal.' I shrugged, grimaced, stroked his cheek for old time's sake, and left.

One of my friends who stayed on said to me next day. 'It was agony – no one knew where to look.' The climax of the evening came when Hakim told them that now he was going to *prove* to them that he was God by hypnotising Halé. 'First he took her in his arms and ran his hands all over her – I thought he was going to fuck her then and there, in front of us all, and she just stood there smiling, you know how she does. Then he made her lie with her head on one chair and her heels on the other, making a stiff bridge between them – you know that old trick. One of the girls screwed up her courage and said she'd seen other people do that too, so did that mean *they* were God, and he went into a rage and began to shout and storm. People were quite frightened. It was a ghastly evening.' A few days later Hakim came into the office to collect some copies of his book and said to me: 'It was a shame you couldn't stay. I hypnotised Halé and everyone was very impressed.'

By then, having quarrelled in some way with the people they went to from my flat, Hakim, Halé and Charlie were staying with Herbert G. Herbert was the drop-out son of a rich German family who had been living in London for several years. While here he had met and married an Indian girl, and they had two small children and no money but what his wife earned in a part-time teaching job. He was a tall, gentle, young man, deep in the process of discovering his own loathing of capitalism, violence, and racism, and the mind-expanding properties of cannabis. Presumably his meeting with Hakim coincided with some critical stage in this process.

His hospitality was generous (though, according to Charlie, not up to much in the way of food) and his admiration was ungrudging, though apparently not quite so straightforward as it appeared to Hakim. I was to ask Herbert later: 'Did *you* believe he was God?' 'No, of course not,' he replied; 'but I thought *his* believing it might be useful.'

Herbert believed himself to be far more 'political' than Hakim. He wanted to act upon society and was thinking in terms of a commune. Believing that Hakim's delusion gave him a magnetic power, he hoped that this power would draw in and hold people. Considering that he went on hoping this after having Hakim to stay for about two months, I can only conclude either that Hakim *did* have magnetic power, or that Herbert was easily misled.

It was Herbert, I think, who discovered that the government of Guyana was prepared to make free grants of land to people who would develop it; and it must have been Hakim who decided that they would raise the money for their passages to Guyana from Herbert's father. Herbert had taken no money from that source for years, and was disinclined to tap it. But by the time I learnt of their plan they were all high on it: they would be off to Germany in a few days, to stay with Herbert's family. Halé had been fighting shy of me for some time, but on that day she came into the office with Hakim and Charlie, and they were all abubble with talk of how they would develop their plot of land into a commune to which oppressed black people from all over the world could come in order to live a free and creative life. Maybe they would start a furniture factory, using the trees cut down as they cleared the land–or maybe, if Herbert's dad would give them some old printing machinery, Hakim would run a school for typesetters. 'In the *Guyanan bush*?' I asked, but such niggling made Hakim impatient. Only Charlie, rather guiltily, confessed (when Hakim couldn't hear him) to having reservations. He was sharing their elation up to a point, because this was a new and even wilder development in his unexpected adventure, but he did confess that he was going to 'wait and see' before committing himself to the voyage, because he couldn't help feeling that 'it may not all be quite so simple as they think'.

By then Hakim had begun to feel that Charlie was something of a drag. I suspected it at the time and Herbert confirmed it later. The game of responsibility had lost its charm and had started to irk him. Shortly before I told him that I would no longer work on his book, he had said to me in an elaborately nonchalant voice, 'I think I must start leaving booze about, to test Charlie.' Hakim genuinely knew a great deal about alcoholism (not surprisingly), and I'd often heard him talk good sense about how to deal with it, so this impulse of wanton irresponsibility horrified me. He backed down when I turned on him for it, but I didn't have much doubt, after that, that Charlie's days as his protegé were numbered. At the moment, however, in the excitement of their new project, the three of them seemed happy together.

Ten

About a month later Halé and Charlie reappeared in London, full of triumph. It had worked! Hakim and Herbert were going straight to Guyana from Germany. Herbert would return for his wife and children when he had sized the situation up, and Halé would join Hakim in Guyana after she had visited his publisher in New York and had 'put his literary affairs in order'. Charlie was heading for Boston and home.

Halé spent only a few minutes with me, but had lost the reserve she had been showing while Hakim's book was being published. She was full of plans to buy a smart dress. 'Americans mind so much about appearances, don't they,' she said. 'If I'm to act as Hakim's agent I must look like they expect an agent to look, so we agreed I must get an elegant black dress.' She thought this comic and wondered how she would feel in such a disguise. 'Like playing in a masquerade,' she said.

Charlie spent an evening with me. He had put on weight – they all had, eating three delicious German meals a day after their months of alarming austerity in London. To start with Herbert's parents had been obviously dismayed by them, but they had rallied and become kind. They lived in a grand and beautiful country house, its walls hung with paintings which Charlie had been made to study for the good of his soul by Herbert's wife. (She had also taken him to the National Gallery while they were in London, and afterwards had confessed a secret longing: she could never tell Herbert, but she had always wanted to have tea in Fortnum and

Mason, so would Charlie take her there now? Nervously they ventured in, drank their pot of china tea, ate their tiny cakes and marvelled with a mixture of horror and thrill at the price. I wish I had been there.) Charlie had loved the peace of the German household – the freshness, the quiet, the birds, the flowers. He made it sound like a kind of paradise. Hakim had endlessly 'debated' Herbert's father, and to great effect. Later Herbert was to tell me, 'He handled my father in a really masterly way'; so either Hakim's 'debating' had improved, or the language difficulty worked in his favour.

The house had a swimming-pool with some kind of lounge or bar attached to it, and Hakim had claimed this as his study, locking everyone out of the pool so that he could work undisturbed. This had annoyed Charlie – it was the first time I'd heard him express annoyance with Hakim. He was, however, full of delight at the way the campaign as a whole had been run. It was a formal household, in which meals were served at fixed times, but 'we soon changed that'. Home-made apple-juice was produced on the estate, and 'we finished off a whole year's supply in three weeks'. 'We really took that place over,' said Charlie happily.

A man, I thought, would have to be very rich indeed if he could afford to pay the fares to Guyana of four adults and two children, simply in order to get rid of unwelcome guests... But perhaps Herbert's dad *was* very rich indeed.

What I asked, was the latest shape taken by the Guyana project?

'Well now – I know you aren't going to like this, Diana, but it's going to be sort of a – what's the word? – a theocracy.'

'Oh *Charlie*!'

'Well...well, yes... But you know, Diana, I still like his ideas. They're *good* ideas...'

Charlie said he felt ashamed of having chickened out, but I was not quite convinced that he had done so. He was very slightly evasive about it, and I thought it possible that Hakim had made it clear that he didn't want him, and that he was saving his face. When he said, 'Perhaps I'll be going down to join them once the thing has got going,' he didn't sound as though he believed it.

After I had said goodbye to him I found myself thinking – or hoping - it just might come off. Hakim had got the money out of Herbert's father, after all, and crazy people do acquire followers and found movements from time to time. What a joke if he did get some kind of community going in Guyana! I would not for one moment have betted on it, but I did allow myself to hope.

Hearsay

I never saw Hakim or Halé again, though I had one
meeting and two telephone conversations with Herbert.
Most of what remains to be told comes from newspaper
reports and from a book called *False Messiah: the story of
Michael X* by Derek Humphry and David Tindall.

About three weeks after they had left for Guyana
Herbert turned up at my office, to say that he was on
his way to collect his wife and children, and could he
please pick up twenty copies of *From the Dead Level*
which Hakim had asked him to take back. I told him
that he would have to pay for them, because Hakim had
already had more copies debited to his account than it
would cover, and Herbert replied that of course he
understood that: he would be getting some money over
the weekend, so if I would call the books in from the
warehouse he'd come by on Monday to collect them
and pay for them. On Monday he nipped in very early
and whisked them away. How he got round our usually
alert receptionist I don't know, because on realising that
I didn't know where he was staying I saw that there was
nothing useful to be done, and felt that there was no
point in making a fuss. Although he had been evasive
and had sounded depressed when I had asked him how
things were going in Guyana, his action suggested that
he and Hakim were still working as a team.

The next time I heard from him, in January 1972, he
was back for good. He told me that their project had
ended in disaster. When he got back to Guyana with his
family he learnt that his friend Hakim Jamal had been
expelled and was now *persona non grata*. I asked what

reason they had given, and he answered by saying miserably that Hakim had behaved like a lunatic from the start. He had 'stopped being serious' the moment they arrived, was unable to concentrate and kept veering from notion to notion – in the morning he'd be talking about the commune, in the evening he'd be full of nonsense about running a chain of cinemas, and worst of all – he insisted on seeking out Guyanese politicians and lecturing them on how to run their country, chiding them for not being good black men. 'So he went madder?' I said, and Herbert answered: 'Oh, he was mad, all right. It's no wonder that Burnham got fed up with him and kicked him out.'

Learning that Hakim and Halé had gone to Trinidad, Herbert had trailed after them and found to his horror that they had taken up with 'that gangster' Michael Malik. Unlike a number of white people, including the novelist Alex Trocchi and John Lennon, Herbert saw at once that Michael was a cynical crook and had no faith in the so-called 'commune' he had established in a private housing development called Christina Gardens at Arima, a small town about twenty miles from Port of Spain. Michael was living in a pleasant house with his wife and children, at the centre of a small, shifting group of young men whom he claimed to be teaching 'self-help'. At first sight it was a peaceful set-up, but in fact Michael was keeping it going – just – by a mixture of bullying, blackmail and conmanship. His 'followers' were recruited from among the unemployed in the poorer quarters of Port of Spain, and included several petty criminals: ignorant, unsophisticated people, easily impressed and dominated. He had been able to create this niche for himself as much because of the shakiness of the host society as because of his own manipulative skills.

Hakim and Halé, said Herbert, were 'more or less living with Michael'. They were in a small bungalow about a hundred yards from his house. Hakim was infatuated with Michael and had decided that he was God.

'But *Hakim* is God!' I said.

'Not now, he isn't. He's given it to Michael.' Herbert's explanation of this transference was that after the humiliating debacle in Guyana Hakim needed to duck responsibility. He had moved them all across the world in such style, and then it had all come to nothing – the role of God had become painful and frightening.

I asked how Halé had taken her God's abdication and he said at first that it must have been a horrible shock for her (and it had in fact distressed her: it was to transpire that she had written an anxious letter to her brother about the effect Michael was having on Hakim). Then Herbert burst out, almost crying: 'But Halé is as bad as he is – maybe even worse.' No sooner had Herbert got there than they had both turned on him, badgering him to get more money from his father. There was no more idealism, no more care for their black brothers, no more teaching, just a flagrant and brutal attempt to force money out of him. They had gone on at him for a whole day – a frightening and evil day. They had become quite different, wanting to do the kind of thing Michael was doing such as charter a plane to fly to Haiti for the cock-fighting, and they were all high on the idea of Voodoo – Michael was going to organise a Voodoo celebration for Hakim. Where had the money for planes come from? He had no idea – Michael was as flat broke as they were, that's why they had been at him so venomously. And later it became worse. Herbert had retreated back to Guyana and Halé was sent after him to continue the persecution. The Guyanan police taped a telephone call she made to Hakim and played it to Herbert: 'Listen – they'd been talking about how to get more money out of me. They'd been talking…they'd been talking about *killing* me! I didn't just leave, I ran away.'

Herbert beat a retreat to Barbados, where he and his family spent a short time 'just resting'. Now he intended to return to his studies in London.

As soon as I heard that Hakim had homed in on Michael Malik I thought, Oh my God, trouble! It seemed to me ominous although there was in fact nothing strange about it. He had been wanting to meet Michael for some time; Michael was there in Trinidad, which is a small place in which it is easy to find anyone you want to see; and Trinidad is also the simplest place to go to if you are suddenly kicked out of Guyana and haven't much money. I was being fanciful when the meeting struck me as having a doomed inevitability – as though something bad which I had always known in my heart would happen had at last come to pass. But I *did* feel like that, and although what the meeting was to lead to would make me feel ill with horror, it was not going to give me any shock of surprise.

Not long after Herbert had given me his news, the Trinidadian police, investigating a fire which had broken out at Michael Malik's house just after he and his family had left for a visit to Guyana, noticed signs in the garden which caused them to dig. They found two recently buried bodies. The first was that of a young Trinidadian, Joseph Skerritt. The second was Halé's. Her body had been there since January 2, Skerritt's since a week or so later.

When this news broke Herbert called me. I said: 'I hope they are going to find Hakim's body too,' and he knew what I meant. Both of us were assuming that if he had not been murdered, then he was among the murderers.

Had he ever shown signs of wanted to be rid of Halé, I asked Herbert, who answered yes. During the months they were all together he had often been so cruel to her that Herbert and his wife had wondered how she could stand it; and an old friend of hers had reported that once she visited him and cried for a long time. I mentioned Hakim's attack on her at his publication party. 'Yes, that kind of thing,' said Herbert. 'But on the other hand I don't see how he could survive without her. He depended on her so much for everything.' And I remembered Hakim saying to her in my presence, 'You know I depend on you as much as you do on me'. I still didn't doubt that those words had been true.

Five men had taken part in Halé's murder, ordered to do so by Michael Malik. Hakim was not one of them: Michael had driven him into Port of Spain on some excuse, to get him out of the way. But it is impossible to believe that Hakim did not know what was planned. Michael had told him that he must get rid of Halé, and when he had protested, as he did at first, had volunteered to 'take the problem off his hands'. He had then instructed Hakim to 'send for someone you can trust', and Hakim (who had often been warned in Boston that Halé would ruin his life) had written to a black Bostonian called Marvin Deane, who now went by the Swahili name 'Kidogo', telling him to come at once. Michael's own killer was a man called Stanley Abbott, but presumably Michael knew that Abbott would be reluctant to kill Halé (as he was). Abbott realised at once that Kidogo had been called in to kill Halé, but was too afraid of Michael to protest – except, weakly, that the stranger was not made to do any of the manual work that went on, whereupon he was told: 'He is a hired killer. A contract man with a lot of experience. He's murdered policemen in Boston and he's not here to use his hands digging in the garden.'

Abbott was to make a full confession to the police, and another of the men involved, Parmassar, was to turn Queen's evidence, so a great deal is known about the killing; but Michael's motive for ordering it remains a matter for speculation. Halé had failed to bring back the money she had been told to wring out of Herbert; she had begun to dislike and distrust Michael; she had once been surprised by him poking about in his study when she thought he was out, and she had angered him by taking photographs of some wood carvings which (although she did not know this) he had stolen. He had told his followers that it was wrong for Hakim to live with a white woman, and he had also told them that she was a spy. But these were no more than triggers. What they released was a lust for murder that was swelling within the man and had reached a point at which it was bound to crack the surface of normality containing it. 'I must have blood' he said to Abbott; and the next murder, that of Joe Skerritt, he was to perform himself with manic violence for no 'reason' at all. After which, in the short time left to him before he was captured, he reacted to anything which displeased him (such as a reminder that payment was due on his house) by threatening to kill.

In Halé's case he seems also to have felt that the spilling of blood would serve as a binding ritual on 'his men'. Their orders were given them the night before. At six o'clock next morning he woke them and set four of them – Abbott, Kidogo, Parmassar and a terrified youth called Chadee – to digging a hole about a hundred yards from his house. The fifth man – his closest henchman, called Steve Yeates – was to call Halé and ask her to come with him in the jeep to fetch the milk, which was collected each morning from a nearby farm. While she was out of the way, Michael fetched Hakim. Someone offered Hakim coffee on his way out, adding, 'What about Halé?', to which he replied 'Halé has gone.' Asked where she had gone, so early in the day, he said, 'She left me.'

Yeates and Abbott had synchronised their watches and Yeates spun out the visit to the farm until the agreed time, when the hole would be ready. The other men were standing round the hole waiting when the jeep arrived back and Yeates reversed it towards them. Abbott called to Halé to come and see what they were doing. The fact that they were holding cutlasses would not have seemed strange to her because the cutlass is an all-purpose tool in Trinidad: she apparently didn't notice that Kidogo had filed the blade of his to a spear-shape. They were a group of people she knew well – Yeates she was said to be fond of – standing in the lovely freshness of that early morning, around dug earth, apparently engaged in the sort of task she often saw them performing. Mildly curious, she moved forward with Abbott at her side. It was he who caught hold of her and jumped with her into the hole. She called out to Yeates: 'Steve, Steve...' but he averted his head, as did both Parmassar and Chadee. Kidogo leapt into the hole and began to chop at her, but she struggled fiercely and his attack was incompetent, covering her arms and body with superficial slashes. Abbott, who was holding her by the neck, started to panic and yelled for somebody to do something, whereupon Yeates ran forward, snatched Kidogo's cutlass and gave her the fatal blow in the throat. Abbott, Kidogo and Yeates scrambled out of the hole, Abbott shouted 'Cover!', and frantically they started to shovel earth over her. She was still alive. When she was covered with about a foot of earth Yeates broke off and went with Chadee to the farm to fetch a load of fresh manure. Abbott and Parmassar, meanwhile, filled in the hole, and then the manure was unloaded on to the grave. The men then went back to Michael's house for a drink of water, during which he telephoned to ask if everything was 'all right'. They sat about outside in a blank silence while Kidogo slowly cleaned his cutlass, and when Michael drove up with Hakim to ask 'Is the tree planted?' they did not answer. Michael's wife and children were there and suspected nothing.

That evening he told the five men: 'You are now members for life and cannot resign.'

Michael Malik was arrested very soon after the discovery of the bodies, having tried to escape across the Guyanese frontier into Brazil. Hakim had left Trinidad before the bodies were found but about three weeks after Halé's death: weeks spent drifting about Christina Gardens, silent and disorientated, doing occasional odd jobs about the place and becoming increasingly afraid of Michael. He wrote a few begging letters to film stars on behalf of the 'commune', and when he and Kidogo returned to Boston was apparently supposed to undertake further fund-raising attempts, and was scared that Michael would somehow pursue him to his death if he failed. He had become a hollow man. Having lost his hold on the personality he had invented for himself, he had nothing: no courage, no pride, no sense.

Immediately after the bodies were found, several interviews with him were published in the British press. They were, of course, declarations of his own innocence, but they were contradictory and unconvincing, and three letters which he wrote me during the following year were crazy. The first begged me to find Halé for him because he was sure that she couldn't really be dead. He said that he had been speaking at the Malcolm X Foundation in Boston one day when Charlie Gooding had come in and handed him a slip of paper on which he'd written 'Halé's body has been found in Michael's garden', but he was unable to believe this. Perhaps she was playing some trick on him and would soon reveal herself, but he felt she was in trouble and he wanted to go to her. If she really was dead he would have to kill himself because he was missing her so badly and it was getting worse every day. Two other people beside myself read that letter, and both of them ended with their faces screwed up in expressions of pain, so strongly did it seem to speak of genuine anguish.

The two later letters were nonsensical rantings against the British for not raising statues to Halé and celebrating her publicly as a heroine and saint. 'Everywhere she went she dignified England. She kept within her the spirit of fair play, sincerity, love, warmth, understanding, knowledge, culture. She radiated; shone with a brightness that had to have been produced in England. It was Halé who carried me past the confused teaching of Malcolm X, not with words but by her conscious deeds, 24 hours a day, every day, day in day out. Call it breeding, call it education, call it whatsoever you will, but for God's sake call it something, give her deeds a name that is worthy of her deeds. Please!' Both letters consisted of several pages of such stuff, including a suggestion that the Queen should give 'some special kind of knighthood' to Halé's mother in recognition of her daughter's 'gallantry and spirit in her concern for her motherland,' and a description of Halé as 'a little English queen stepping out to face the world.' A windy rattle of absurdity.

It seemed astonishing that Hakim was not charged, or at least summoned as a witness, when Michael and the others came to trial, but I learnt later that the prosecution had so much conclusive evidence against Michael and his men that they didn't think it worth bothering about him. They knew he had not been present at the killing, and whether or not he was implicated in any other way did not interest them. Kidogo, on the other hand, they wanted, and they knew where he was: he and Hakim were moving about Boston quite openly together. The Trinidad police were, however, prevented by a legal technicality from having him extradited. American law regarding extradition lays down that the wanted person must be identified in court by a witness from the country where that person is alleged to have committed the crime. Except for Michael Malik's wife who could not be unprejudiced, all the witnesses who knew Kidogo in Trinidad were either dead or convicted of capital crimes.

The men condemned to death for Halé's murder were Abbott and Chadee. Steve Yeates had died from drowning, somewhat mysteriously, before the bodies were found; Parmassar got off by turning Queen's evidence; Kidogo was snug in Boston; and Michael Malik had already received the death sentence for the murder of Joe Skerritt, so the charge against him in Halé's case was 'kept in reserve'.

Hakim once described to me what he called 'the worst night' of his life, which happened when he and his wife Dorothy were breaking up over Jean. After a terrible row Dorothy left the house, taking the children, and when Hakim was going to bed he discovered that his gun was gone from under it, where he always kept it. He concluded that jealousy of Jean had driven Dorothy out of her mind and knew that she meant to come back in the night and shoot him as he slept. He put a hard chair in a corner of the room where a bullet through the window couldn't reach, and sat up on it all night, not letting himself doze off, thinking all the time that he could hear her outside.

In the packet of Jean's letters which he left with me there were a few from other women including one from Dorothy – the one in which she said that in the past he had not been so bad as all that. She referred to that night. It was that night which decided her that she couldn't take him back. 'To think,' she said 'that it would ever come to me having to ask the police for protection against you.' It seemed from this that she had taken the gun because she feared that *he* had gone insane and would use it on her. I doubt, however, that Hakim was deliberately lying when he gave me his version: there was no reason why he should. He had volunteered the story as one against himself, an example of how hard he had been on Dorothy, driving her to desperation. He was confessing to unmanly panic in a situation which he blamed himself for creating. I think he was remembering the night as he described it – perhaps had even *experienced* it like that. Having read Dorothy's letter I concluded that if an event had been specially stressful to Hakim – if it had loaded him with a guilt which he found intolerable – then his account of it would be false not because he was lying but because he had changed it into something else in his own mind. Clearly, no one could learn from what Hakim *said* the truth about what made him fall in with Michael's plan to kill Halé, or what he felt about it afterwards; and I doubt if the truth would have become any more apparent had it been possible to read his thoughts.

On May 1 1973, a year and four months after Halé's death, Hakim was dead in Roxbury. The two deaths were unconnected. Hakim had settled in Roxbury, living with another white woman to whom he gave the name Hané (did he think that Halé's soul had taken possession of her body?), and together with Kidogo had joined in various community projects. One of these was run by a group called De Mau Mau which had originated in Vietnam among the marines. At their peak there were four hundred of them, acting as community police to protect blacks, and imposing their own justice when the real police could not or would not operate. Hakim disagreed with some of their ideas, but this does not seem to have been why five of them burst into his apartment one evening when he was there with Hané, Kidogo and two other friends. His dog attacked them on the stairs and was shot. Hakim jumped up, grabbed for his gun and was also shot. One of the attackers was to say later that they had really come to take Kidogo back to their headquarters in order to 'implement Black Law' because he had insulted one of their women, but Kidogo was unharmed. Hakim's death was as empty of meaning as his life had become.

I felt no sorrow when I heard of it; there was even a sensation of relief.

But as the days passed, sadness emerged – not that he was dead, but that his dangerousness and his end had been laid down for him by the conditions of his birth and couldn't be escaped, although he tried. He was trying when he became a follower of Malcolm X, struggling to help not only himself but also others like himself. He was trying even when he 'became God'. I remembered him sitting here in my flat, tasting kindness and peace with so much pleasure. I remembered that in short flashes he was able to exercise an exceptional gift for kindness and peace, creating memorable islands of them for those he was with. I remembered his talk of those happy times in Morocco, walking back from the beach with Halé, their mouths 'going a mile a minute', and the evenings when they left their door open even though approaching footsteps made their hearts sink because they were so contented together. The open door was his response to the open kindness of their neighbours, and when he spoke of that his face changed as though he were inwardly savouring something beautiful. Once, when we were talking about attempts to desegregate schools in the South, he suddenly cried out, his face twisted with a kind of puzzled sorrow, 'How can there be so little *kindness*?' I remembered how he 'died' to kiss the soft, gentle-looking face of his lovely almost-white mother, and how he kissed my face so tenderly, as though in a dream of loving. If Hakim had not wanted so desperately ('in the *worst* way') to embrace kindness, beauty, security – everything snatched away from him by his mother and denied him by the white people she resembled – he would not have been a man who caused death and who ended by being killed.

Hakim was a loving child unloved, a beautiful child made to believe he was ugly, a clever child starved into a process of desperate self-invention, and he was condemned to live from the day he was born among people many of whom had been shaped in much the same way that he had been. Thinking of that, grief and horror grow stronger, not less, with the passing of time.

STET

An Editor's Life

For nearly five decades Diana Athill helped shape some of the
finest books in modern literature. She edited (and nursed and
coerced and coaxed) some of the most celebrated writers in the
English language, including V. S. Naipaul, Jean Rhys, Norman
Mailer and Brian Moore. This candid and truthful memoir
writes 'stet' against the pleasures, intrigues and complexities of
her life spent among authors and manuscripts.

'A little gem . . . nostalgic, funny and valuable, written
unashamedly for those who care about books' *Observer*

'This is a memoir of a life in publishing, and is written with a
lovely and elegant lucidity' *Daily Telegraph*

'A narrative in which the passing literary stars take second
place to an extraordinary guiding intelligence – sceptical,
amused, humane' *New Statesman*

AFTER A FUNERAL

When Diana Athill met the man she calls Didi, an Egyptian in exile, she fell in love instantly – and out of love just as fast. Instead they became friends. Didi moved into her flat, they shared housework and holidays, and a life of easy intimacy seemed to beckon.

But Didi's sweetness and intelligence soon revealed a darker side – he was a gambler, a drinker and a womanizer, impossible to live with but impossible to ignore. With tender, painful honesty Diana Athill explores the three years they spent together; a period that culminated in Didi's suicide – in her flat – an event he described as 'the one authentic act of my life'.

'Anyone who believes that human relationships are important cannot fail to be moved by this book' *Daily Telegraph*

'A book which gives a new dimension to honesty, a new comprehension to love' *Vogue*

YESTERDAY MORNING
A Very English Childhood

In *Yesterday Morning* Diana Athill looks back on a childhood unfashionably filled with happiness – a Norfolk country house, servants, the pleasures of horses, the unfolding secrets of adults and sex. This is England in the 1920s, seen from the vantage point of England in 2001. It was a privileged and loving life, but did it equip her to be happy?

'Athill's honesty in describing her feelings as a young girl and an old woman makes her memoir universal. The humiliations of being young, the fear of looking silly, will strike a chord with anyone who remembers growing up' *Independent*

'The work of a writer happy to luxuriate in a vanished past, which she now credits with giving her everything that made possible her later survival. However, there is nothing false about the retrospection, and you believe every word she writes. Unmarried, childless and precise by nature, Diana Athill has no reason not to tell the truth' *Daily Telegraph*

DON'T LOOK AT ME LIKE THAT

In England half a century ago, well-brought-up young women are meant to aspire to the respectable life. Some things are not to be spoken of; some are most certainly not to be done. There are rules, conventions. Meg Bailey obeys them. She progresses from Home Counties school to un-Bohemian art college with few outward signs of passion or frustration. Her personality is submerged in polite routines; even with her best friend, Roxane, what can't be said looms far larger than what can.

But circumstances change. Meg gets a job and moves to London. Roxane gets married to a man picked out by her mother. And then Meg does something shocking. Shocking not only by the standards of her time, but of our own.

'She has added importantly to those works of literature which illuminate the vagaries of human emotion' *Daily Telegraph*